Marketing as Ministry

It's Not About Your or Your Book

by Cheri Cowell

with Michelle Booth

Marketing as Ministry

Published by EA Books Publishing a division of
Living Parables of Central Florida, Inc. a 501c3
EABooksPublishing.com

Dedication

To our Lord, who was the best marketer who ever lived—from a handful of true believers to a movement that is still changing the world. May we learn to serve as you served with the gifts we've been given, and then leave the results in your capable hands.

Acknowledgements

We'd like to thank the staff of EABooks Publishing—the BEST staff in all of the publishing world (we may be biased). You serve our authors with integrity and excellence, and you honor God in everything you do.

We'd both like to thank our husbands who support us as we follow our calling.

Finally, we'd like to thank all of the authors who have trusted us with your book babies and your ministries. It has been a privilege to serve you and help you reach the world for God's glory.

Contents

Introduction   vii

Chapter 1: If It's Not About Me, Then What?   1

    The Two Big Questions
    Uniquely Gifted & Qualified
    Cake & Icing

Chapter 2: Your Foundation—Your Cake   7

    Questions to Consider
    Driving Traffic
    What Does Your Brand Say?

Chapter 3: Platform—Connecting to Your Readers   27

    Social Media
    Email Marketing
    Blogs
    Amazon Author Page

Chapter 4: The Best Time to Start Marketing   47

    The Most Important Decision
    While You Are Still Writing
    Blueprint for Action
    Think

Chapter 5: Icing the Cake   73

    Evergreen Articles
    Book Launch Plan
    Online Book Clubs
    Traditional Book Tours
    Media Tours

Newspapers
Current Event Expert

Chapter 6: Business Basics   95

Business Card
Headshot
Bios
Hashtags
Press Release
Media Kit
Business Plan

Chapter 7: Indie, Self, Co – Oh My!   105

Types of Publishing
Going Hybrid
Traditional vs. Independent

Chapter 8: Questions to Ask Yourself   117

What Is Your Why?
Who Is This For?
Who Has Your Rights?
Should You DIY?
Questions to Ask before You Sign a Contract
Change Your Mindset
Common Causes of Failure

Chapter 9: A Word of Encouragement   139

Start Small
Overwhelmed?
Join Hands

Appendix   145

Living Parables of Central Florida   175

Introduction

It's Not About You

For seven years before getting my first book contract, I attended two to three writers' conferences a year. I took copious notes in every marketing class, and when I returned from these conferences, I was a good little student. I followed the directions I was given and did *everything* they told me to do. *Everything!*

The result: I spun my wheels in a million different directions and spent a ton of money. I had some successes, but I also failed miserably. One day after tweeting, posting, blogging, and writing marketing copy, I finally said to God, "There has to be a better way." His response was, "Yes, there is. Are you willing to listen now?" I thought, *Yes, I'm willing to listen because I am worn out.*

During the next six months the Lord and I went through an immense process. I took my notes and handouts from the conferences and covered my office floor with them. I put them in stacks. I made notes, diagrams, and outlines. As the Lord and I worked together, the main message I kept hearing from

Him was, "Marketing is not about you. This is not about you." But my notes appeared to be about my book and me. So how could this be about my book and me, and then not be about me? I wrestled with this, much like Jacob wrestling with God in the Bible. By the end of the six months God showed me some incredible things. Now I will share these things with you.

In *Marketing as Ministry*, we will discuss what you need to know before you publish your book, and we'll cover what you can do while you are still writing so you can be more successful when you get to the publishing stage.

We'll talk about your target market and about proposals. Finally, we'll talk about the investments and resources you will need to be successful. I will share with you the answers the Lord gave me during those six months of marketing training by the best Marketer of all time.

These concepts apply whether you plan to publish one book or multiple books. These are the same concepts whether you go the traditional or independent publishing route. In fact, they are the same concepts used in most successful marketing endeavors when Christians are in the driver's seat. They are at the heart of what Jesus did when He showed the disciples what to do to spread the gospel message.

I'm going to share my trade secrets with you. They are part of the marketing coaching package my publishing company offers. You might wonder why I would do this when this is what people pay us for. The answer is, I believe we are all on the same team, and if I can help you—God wins.

So grab an author friend—someone who will be honest and vulnerable with you, someone you can be vulnerable with and work through these concepts with—or you can hire one of our marketing coaches who will do this with you in an organized, methodical manner. Either way, you will find it helpful to have a sounding board for all of the ideas you'll be coming up with as you read this book, because marketing is not about you or your book. Now let's find out why.

Chapter 1

If It's Not About Me, Then What?

I have coached authors one-on-one and conducted marketing retreats for more than a decade. The biggest struggle I see authors face when it comes to marketing their book is a feeling of selfishness. We know in our hearts we are not supposed to be self-promoters, and yet everything appears to be all about "me" and all about "my book." When you and I see a person marketing themselves and their book, we feel an aversion to that and we don't want to be one of "those people." Innately, we know it's not about us. So how do we marry the idea that we need to market ourselves and our book with the idea that it's not about us?

The Two Big Questions

This is what God shared with me during those six months while I was sitting on my office floor. This is where the magic comes in. For us as Christians, we believe God has given us a unique message for a unique set of people. For instance, maybe you are writing a book on grief. There are hundreds of books out there on grief. So you begin by exploring how your message is different. Identify what needs you are speaking to in the life of your reader, and what makes you gifted and qualified to speak to those needs.

To help you do this, the first question I want you to answer is, "What are my readers' hopes, dreams, fears, and faith questions?" Let's continue with the grief example. You might respond, "This book is for someone who is grieving." Noooo. That answer is too broad. It's a starting point, but you need to take it further and get more specific.

Let's consider the question again. If your reader is someone who is grieving, what is one of his or her fears? They might feel that they are being swallowed alive by their grief and they fear they won't be able to get out of the deep hole that they're in. That's a fear and it is real.

Now turn that fear question around to you as the author for the second question: How are you uniquely gifted and qualified to speak to that fear? You are writing your book because you have experienced that period of grief and you know what it's like to be in that dark hole. You know what it feels like to not see a way out. What did you learn as you transitioned from your deep despair to where you are now? What did you learn that will speak to your readers' fear?

Maybe you learned that the ladder that gets you out of grief is climbed by reaching up to someone else who is reaching a hand down to help you—someone who has climbed their way up that same ladder and who now wants to help you do the same. You learned to look up to somebody who has found the light.

Take out a legal pad and on separate pages create your headings: My Readers' Hopes, My Readers' Dreams, My Readers' Fears, and My Readers' Faith Questions. Spend some time building your lists. Draw from your experience and do some research.

I am a Bible study teacher so one of the fears I address in my books is, "I have dumb questions." There are people who don't understand some basic concepts and they think everybody else understands. These people don't want to look dumb so they don't ask the simple questions in Sunday school class or in Bible study. They have questions like, "Salvation sounds like something important but it doesn't make sense. How can it be a free gift at the same time that Jesus paid the price for it?" As the author, I'm going to answer some basic questions in my books so people don't fear looking stupid.

Uniquely Gifted & Qualified

Now I want you to make a list of how you are gifted and qualified to address your readers' fears, hopes, dreams, and faith questions. If you're serious about working through this process, it should take three weeks to build your stream of consciousness lists. At the end of the three weeks, when there are no more ideas coming, find either a friend or a coach to help you review your lists. This is the exciting part—when I work with authors, this is when the light bulb comes on—you will begin to see themes developing. These themes are the core messages you will communicate as you promote your book. They are what will drive your marketing campaign. Your core messages are what will resonate with your readers.

Can you see what is happening at this point? You are turning your marketing into ministry. You are ministering to the needs your readers have with the messages God has given you. You are no longer talking about you. You are no longer talking about your book. You're meeting people's needs, and that is where ministry happens.

Cake & Icing

Remember how I attended all of those marketing classes and how I was a good little student? I went home and did everything they taught me to do, and I was spinning my wheels in a million different directions. Well, I love it when I work with writers who feel the same way. I have been where they are and I understand how they feel. I love that I can use what I have learned to help them stop spinning their wheels and find a path forward.

There are so many opportunities for authors to market their books: radio, articles, newspapers, the internet, and Facebook, to name a few. The problem is, you and I are only one person. We can't do everything all at once. Some authors start by focusing on the icing — media appearances, speaking engagements, book signings — all of the marketing strategies that seem like fun. However, unless you have already baked your cake, there is no need for the icing.

At EABooks we teach authors the concept of making the cake first and then adding the icing at the right time. In practical terms, that means you need to start by creating a website. And your website needs to be reader-focused, not author-focused. It needs to meet your readers' needs, not be filled with content that is all about you and your book.

We also use the analogy of building a house. You can't put the roof on a home until you have built the foundation and the walls. The foundation is your website. It is what everything else is built on.

Once you have your website built, the walls go up next. Your walls are the basics of social media. Again, social media is not going to be about you or your book. It's going to be about your reader. Finally, after you've built the foundation and the walls, you're ready for that roof. Let's take a look at what goes into building your foundation.

Chapter 2

Your Foundation — Your Cake

Using the analogy of baking a cake, your website is the cake and your other marketing tactics make up the frosting. When I attended all of those writers' conferences, one of the things they told me I needed was a website, and a million other things. I'll get to the million other things in later chapters, but when it came to building my website I did a few things right and a lot of things wrong. The problem with building a website is you don't know what you don't know. And I didn't know a lot.

To begin with, I hired someone who hung out a Christian shingle, yet his business practices were not very Christ-like. Second, I spent a lot of money for him to create my site and then every time I needed him to make an update, I had to pay for that, too. Thirdly, I learned this person had a lot of other clients and I was not a priority. Unless I was paying for him to redo my entire website, none of my minor changes were made quickly. In our industry, your website needs to change constantly, and I wasn't able to make that happen with this vendor.

Many authors think that just having a website means readers will find them. They use an "If I build it, they will come" mentality. To help you avoid some of my mistakes, and to make your website a destination that readers want to find and spend time at, you need to ask yourself: Is my website . .

. . . My Name or My Book Title?

The first question you will need to answer when you're setting up your website is what your domain name will be. You have a few choices. You can use your name, the title of your book — if you only plan on writing one book — or it can be related to your core message or ministry. This is where having a marketing coach is helpful, to think through these questions. Then do a domain name search to see if the name you're thinking of using has already been taken. This will often eliminate some options.

. . . A Custom Site, or Another Type?

Another consideration as you're planning your website is what type of site is best for your situation. Your first option is a DIY site. If you go this route, find an online website builder, choose a template that you like, add your content, and you're ready to go.

A semi-custom website, which is what we use at EABooks for our authors, is another option. Our two favorite website builders are 1and1 and SquareSpace, but there are many others to choose from. Our marketing coaches work with authors to set up their account, select a template, and design the site. Then they coach authors on how to use the site so they can update it and make changes on their own.

Your third option is a custom website. If there are a lot of bells and whistles you need on your site, then this is a good way to go. Custom sites are going to start around $2,500 and go up from there depending on how sophisticated your design and functionality must be. I suggest starting with a DIY site or hiring someone who can help you create the site and then coach you on how to use it. Your local Christian Writers' Conference is the place to get names of people you can trust.

If you're looking at doing it yourself or going with a semi-custom site, you can expect to pay around $500 to $800. Of course, the rates increase with the more bells and whistles you add, such as a custom shopping cart or flash for videos.

. . . Reader-Focused?

Ten, fifteen, even twenty years ago, author websites were author-focused. You went to an author's website to read about the author. But a shift in the industry has occurred. People are bombarded with information on the internet, and they are no longer interested in visiting a website to learn about someone else. The reason people would want to come to your website is because it holds answers to their questions (those questions you're uniquely qualified to address, that you identified in Chapter 1).

A website is a destination where, when readers go there, they say to themselves, "This person gets me. This person speaks my language. This person has answers I'm looking for and solutions to my problems." That is what a website is supposed to do. It does not need to be expensive. It doesn't need to be complicated. It does not need to be difficult for you as an author to maintain. It does need to be reader-focused.

Questions to Consider

I want you to picture a highway in Los Angeles. It is fourteen lanes across and jam-packed with cars traveling eighty miles an hour. You want them to get off at your exit— to go to your website located along this Information

Superhighway. If they were speeding down this superhighway, why would they choose your exit?

As you envision this highway, think about the person who is driving eighty miles an hour—your reader. Now consider this question: Who is that person, what are they doing that day, and why are they on the Information Superhighway?

The next question is what is causing them to look for a site like yours. Are they stressed? Are they worried? Are they looking for answers to a problem they need to solve? What is going on in their life? Are they looking for hope, a friend, peace, or joy? What exactly are they looking for?

Once you have the answer to that question, you will develop your website around those key-words contained in your answers. If you know they're looking for joy, then your website content needs to be playful and joyful. The design needs to have splashes of color and it needs to be fun. It needs to be full of life and energy. This is what will speak to your reader. If, however, the keywords for your website are about peace, you don't want to create the website to be joy-focused.

Understanding why people are coming to your site is key to building a reader-focused website. Knowing what is driving them there is not only going to help you, but if you are working with a website designer, it will help the designer to customize the landing page and the entire website—the layout and the content—to meet your readers' needs.

Ministry in Action–Bob Ousnamer, Marketing Coach

One of the most fun challenges in building a website is determining the content for each page of the site. The rule that less is more applies here. Each page should create the desire of the reader to know more. How many times do you see "Learn More" or "Go Further" on a website or social media post? Our tendency to tell everything we know in the first two minutes of a conversation does not always serve us well, especially in the ethereal world of the internet.

In one of our most recent website builds, we were working with an author whose book dealt with recovering addicts. Not only had she written a Bible study, she was also involved in a number of local ministries that served her community. There were many different elements that needed to come together in a cohesive manner to compel the reader of the website to learn more.

In our discussions about her domain name, we decided to work with (her name)ministries.com. Fortunately, that domain was available and so we proceeded to add it to her cart as well as purchase the base website hosting package. Our website host normally offers a free one-year subscription for a domain name when purchased with the hosting package. The first-year cost for this author's website was $11.82—quite a bargain!

Earlier discussions helped determine her target audience, and the bulk of the web content was ready to copy and paste into the website templates. It is important to remember that, even though they appear to be complete templates, everything is malleable within the template. Text boxes, images, and other elements can be arranged in a variety of visual presentations.

The author wanted a number of visual images combined with scriptural texts to adorn the sight. We spent some time searching the internet for non-copyrighted or common copyright images. There are many available, and we selected a half dozen and joined scripture with each one. This material was then added to an animated banner at the top of the home page to work as an attractive welcoming platform. The banner was also duplicated at the bottom of some other pages. Three short paragraphs were added to describe the purpose of the site (ministry). Below that we added four columns that duplicated some of the navigation tabs at the top of the screen. This would give the reader two opportunities on the home page to skip to more in-depth material: The Book, The Author, News & Reviews, and Contact Us. At the bottom of the page in the footer, we added links to her social media (Facebook, Twitter, and blog) along with links to the three local ministry websites she is involved with. This footer would then be available on every page within the site.

The author decided that she would like to try blogging. She felt that her subject material and involvement in the community would work well on this platform. We created a free blog at Blogsite.com, a Google-based platform. The blog site also used templates, and we selected one that would complement the branding on her website. After posting her first blog, we added a blog page to the website and linked the RSS feed to it. This allows her to respond and collect information regarding visitors and comments on her blog postings, helping build her online community.

We also discussed ideas for a logo for her ministry. The author envisioned a hawk soaring over high mountains.

There are a myriad of soaring hawks and eagles on the internet, but distilling that to a logo isn't always easy. I was able to find two royalty-free images that could be edited to create a hawk soaring above a jagged mountain, set in a rectangle with a light blue sky and gray/brown mountain — very plain, very descriptive. Simple and elegant, it could be used as a color image or black and white relief on letterhead, emails, pins, stationery, products, etc. We placed it at the top center of each web page as a small image to create continuity.

Driving Traffic

Now that you understand why people are looking for a website like yours, how are you going to get people to visit your specific website? We've all driven by people standing on the corner who are flipping and twirling those signs to call attention to a sale or a grand opening or some other promotion. If you don't want to stand there all day and flash a sign, there are other ways to get people to notice your exit. I'm going to use some traffic terminology to discuss the different ways of driving traffic to your website.

GPS

Everyone today seems to have some form of a GPS. For authors, the GPS is the keywords you will use when you create your website. If you've already set up a website, you might have thrown in a few words not realizing how important they are. Google uses these words to direct people to your website. These words are not the words that appear on your website, they are keywords written in code behind the scenes.

How do you identify the right keywords? I suggest you plug in a few of them and run a Google search. See what websites pop up. Are they similar to yours or do they direct people to content that is not closely enough aligned with what you are hoping to provide for your readers?

"Fear" might be one of the keywords you want to use on your website. If somebody types, "fear" or "dealing with fear" into Google, what other websites come up? Would your website be an answer for people in that category? When you put in these keywords, other keywords will pop up. I suggest you spend a couple of weeks doing these kinds of searches. You will end up with a long list of words that are linked. You can also use a thesaurus with synonym and antonym finders to identify keywords that are similar to what you are searching for.

Directional Signs

Directional signs for an author are not big billboards, but those smaller signs on the side of the road that say, "Cracker Barrel 5 Miles." They are commonly referred to in the internet world as algorithms. This is a complicated process, but basically algorithms are what will make Google point to your website over the other websites that are like yours. You accomplish that by building on the things that will improve your Google ranking. This is called playing the algorithms.

One way to improve your Google ranking is to link to other sites that are like yours. Because CheriCowell.com focuses on those who are leading Bible studies and those who are interested in knowing more about their Bibles, I link to several websites of authors who are also writing good Bible content. They write blogs, sell books, or offer resources I think are good for those who are interested in Bible study.

You might wonder why I would suggest pointing people to other websites when you want them to stay on yours. We're back to the concept of "We are all on the same team, and if I can help you—God wins." The more you link arms with other people who are doing what you're doing, it builds their readership, and your readers are grateful you are sending them to other sites that will help them in their search. It's not taking away from you; it's actually building your readership. It's another way to keep your website reader-focused. It's also helping to build those algorithms that will increase your Google ranking.

Before you link to other sites, a good practice is to send an email to these fellow authors first. Let them know you will be linking to their website through your website, and if they feel it would be beneficial to their readership to link to your website, you would appreciate the return gesture. You don't need to wait for an approval before including a link on your website. If they should reciprocate, it increases that Google ranking. That's a good practice.

Off-Ramps

This is a fun one. Off-ramps are hyperlinks to your other online content not located directly on your website. Let's say you are going to write a guest blog on another author's website. At the bottom of your guest blog post, in your signature line, you will include a hyperlink to your website. Then when you link to that guest blog post from your website, the link will increase your Google ranking. It will also provide an off-ramp so the reader who finishes reading that guest blog post and clicks on your link will be taken directly to your website. You would do this same thing for any articles you publish for online outlets. The bio at the end of your article will include a hyperlink to your website.

Billboards

Similar to a big billboard on the highway that drives traffic to a specific destination, your billboard to drive traffic to your website is your social media. In the next chapter I will go into detail about using social media for your marketing. What I want you to understand for now is that social media is not about what you had for lunch or where you went on vacation. Social media is your billboard, enticing people to exit the highway and go to your website. Just like a billboard on the highway with pictures of food or a mega shopping outlet with great stores, they are meant to make the traveler want to take that exit and go check it out. Social media connects to a need, builds a relationship, generates curiosity, or offers something valuable so the reader says, "Let me go check that out."

What Does Your Brand Say?

When you begin working on your website, whether it's a DIY, semi-custom, or custom site (I'll discuss these options in more detail in a later chapters), an important aspect to think about is the look. The colors, fonts, logo, tag line — all of these things will say visually what you are also saying in word.

The look of your website needs to match the reason why people are coming to your website. Again, if your website is about joy, you need to use bright, happy colors. If your website is mainly to help your reader with peace, you need to use calming colors, and a font that is easy on the eye and instills peace in the reader just by looking at it. All of this is combined into what forms your brand.

Go back to why your reader would take your exit off of the Information Superhighway. Once you have the answer to that question, the rest of this information will help create your brand. You will extend the branding to all of your other marketing efforts as well, so that everything works together to support your themes and core messages you identified in Chapter 1.

CheriCowell.com is geared toward people who are interested in the Bible—teaching, exploring, or who have questions about the Bible—this is my core constituency. When I was thinking about the tag line for my website, the thing that kept coming to my mind was "I'm a Bible study teacher and I am a United Methodist." John Wesley was the founder of Methodism and his label was an armchair theologian. He was not a highfalutin theologian from the scholarly standpoint, but rather he took theology and applied it to everyday life. I've always loved that and identified with that because that is my area of giftedness. This is where I connect to my readers. I wanted to do a little bit of play on words, so I am Cheri Cowell, author, speaker, and sidewalk theologian.

When someone comes to my website and they see that tag line, those that are of the Wesleyan tradition will recognize the armchair and sidewalk theologian as being similar and wonder if I share their theology. They will explore my website and find that I do.

Those who do not have my theology background will wonder what sidewalk theologian means. They will explore my website and find that I take the complicated things of faith and share them as if I'm standing on the sidewalk of life talking about the things of faith with a friend. That's how I wanted my website to feel.

The colors, fonts, the look, and even the lamb that is the image in the header on my website all speak to that theme and that feeling. That's what I mean when I talk about a brand. That lamb has become my brand; the sidewalk theologian is an integral part of who I am, what my brand says about me, and the message I'm sharing.

You're going to want to do the same thing. This is again where the coaching concept can be helpful. It's a lot easier to develop your brand when you have someone to bounce ideas off of. That sidewalk theologian tag line did not come easily. It came through a series of brainstorming sessions with a coach. It is the same method we use at EABooks Publishing.

Ministry in Action–John Copeland, Marketing Coach

Branding is having a logo — but it's much more. It's . . .

- Who *you* are: Figure out who you are, what you do best and how you can offer it to the world.

- Who *they* are: Build a community. Ask questions within that community in regards to your area of expertise. What are their needs? What can you give away? Share your background story. *Become* a member of the community, offer hope, and meet their needs by what you offer.

- *What* you portray: Create a "look" or a "brand" with colors, font, imagery and a logo that stays consistent with everything your business does.

Your brand identity is really about how your audience perceives you. Hence, why figuring out what you can offer your audience is of vital importance. Then, when a customer visits your website (or social media page), your color choices, fonts, imagery, and the mood it portrays, send a message of who you are and what you offer them.

Here are examples of five marketing clients we've worked with and how their font, imagery, and color choices helped to create a mood on their website.

- One client we worked with is a caring and soft-spoken devotional author, and a strong prayer warrior. For her book cover, logo, and website design, we chose a soft, green sapling cradled by a hand, springing forth from a stark black and white background, signaling new growth. We chose the feminine and trending Playlist Script font.

- Another author knows many Christians in her community who have fallen away from their faith. Her passion became inner-city rebirth and the resurgence of faith. We used the graffiti-like font Edo with black, gray, white, and red. In her words, "the black signifies death, the red, Christ's blood, and pure white was the life after rededication to Christ."

- We have another client who ministers to women who are feeling hopeless due to circumstances in their lives that are beyond their control. They need comfort and hope in Christ. We chose the feminine Sacramento font, a butterfly (new birth), and soothing peach colors.

- For our client who loves to use imagery on her website, we worked together to find pictures that effectively portrayed her message, were available, and were either free or affordable on the internet.

- One author had written a superhero graphic novel. We wanted his font to stay consistent with what was used in his book, so we chose Comic Pro. Because his main character was a superhero, red and black were the strong colors of choice.

- We also worked with a cheerful grandma who is perfect for writing children's books. She was thrilled with the adorable illustrations our illustrator created for her, so we used a particular depiction for her logo. The colors were taken from the illustration as well, and we chose fonts that were whimsical and easy to read.

As you can see, branding varies greatly, depending on what the author offers, the audience, and the message. The key is to take your branding elements and keep them consistent throughout your website, social media, letterhead, mailing list, and any other area that conveys your message.

Chapter 3

Platform — Connecting to Your Readers

At one of the conferences I attended as a writer, they said we needed to be on social media to build our platform. They explained the platform is how we connect to readers and that social media was the newest and biggest thing. So, like the good little soldier that I am, I went home and created a Facebook account and a Twitter account. At the end of the day, I laid my head on my pillow and realized I had forgotten to post anything. *I'll do it tomorrow*, I told myself. At the end of the next day, I laid my head on the pillow and realized I had forgotten to post again. Okay, *I'll do it tomorrow*, I told myself.

At the end of the first week I had not posted a thing. I'm a little bit older and I like to say, "My hip bone is not connected to my cell phone." When something great happens in my life, my first thought is to call my mother, not post about it on Facebook. Social media was not a part of my life and I knew I needed to figure out how to make it work for me.

Social Media

Although people on social media are called your friends, many of them are not the people you actually see or speak to on a regular basis. They are not the people you would call in a crisis. However, for those of us who are not thrilled about jumping on the social media bandwagon, I have come to learn that it does have a place for us as authors.

As we've discussed in the previous chapters, your marketing should not be about you or your book. This includes your social media posts. You should not talk about what you had for dinner or where you are vacationing on Facebook and Twitter unless that is a part of your brand. I recommend a different approach, and it is what the marketing coaches at EABooks use.

When we sit down with an author, we work with them to develop a social media plan that addresses their readers' hopes, dreams, fears, and faith questions. We want their social media to point people to the author's website, because their website is where their ministry is taking place. Don't look at your website as a place where you're selling books, but rather where you're ministering to people's needs.

We want to be the kind of authors who people want to follow and engage with. The key with social media is changing your mindset to how you can serve others. That is how you can incorporate social media into your ministry. This Christian principle applies everywhere else, so why would it not apply with our social media?

Content

When I set up my social media accounts and kept forgetting to post anything that first week, I knew I needed to find a way to integrate social media into my life. I'm a to-do list type of gal, so I found it helpful to create a social media plan. If you're just getting started with social media, I recommend you do the same. Start with five days of a week and brainstorm a list of five categories of content you can give away to your readers—things they are looking for that only you can provide, such as resources, knowledge, and inspiration.

Share your expertise as a writer and the research that you've used to write your book, and reuse it to minister to other people on social media. Look at what other authors in your genre are posting about, then begin by making a list of all the things people will come to your website to receive. I recommend you make a list of five things. Why five? There are five days in a week and if you post once every day for five days, you are among the top five social media users. Think: What can I give away? What value can I provide?

Ministry in Action–Cheri Cowell

For me, I chose: 1. Quotes from famous theologians; 2. Scriptures for various purposes such as seeking wisdom; 3. Faith questions—sometimes I pose the question and sometimes I answer the question; 4. Resources for ministry leaders—this includes linking to other blogs, articles I've written or others have written, or Bible study tools; and 5. Giveaways on my own website such as tip sheets, resource sheets, and other downloads.

Think about the days of the week in other ways. For instance, Thursday on Facebook is called "Throwback Thursday." If you participate in Throwback Thursday that means you post an old picture from your family, your childhood, or something else from the past on Thursday. But why are you doing this? When I participate in Throwback Thursday it is always about leaving a legacy of faith and standing on the shoulders of the Great Cloud of Witnesses. Always tie what you are posting to your core message and what your readers are looking for from you. Another idea would be Scripture Saturday when you could post all of those scriptures you compiled as research for your book.

You might decide you want to post every other day instead of every day. Whatever schedule you want to follow is fine, as long as it's consistent.

Outlets

Facebook is the big granddaddy on the block. It is a place where people connect with others who are of like mind and interests. When you publish content on Facebook—the quotes, research, scripture, tips from your social media plan—it is called a post.

If you have a personal Facebook account, the people you are connected with are considered friends whether you actually know them or not. You can also set up a professional page, but instead of connecting with friends, you will invite people to "like" this page.

If you already have a Facebook page under your name with posts all about your family and your vacations and who got potty-trained, I encourage you to set up a different Facebook page for your professional persona. You will need to use a slightly different name for your professional page like your full name with your middle initial, or your full name followed by "Author."

If you have a personal Facebook account and then you set up your professional account, you need to publish a

Facebook post on your personal page announcing you've started a new Facebook account for your professional writing career, and invite people to like and follow your professional page. You can use the transition process available from Facebook, and then all of your current friends will be "ported over" to your new page. The nice thing about sending the message out on your personal Facebook page is, this tells your family that you're not going to be bugging them about buying your book. They will appreciate that.

Twitter is basically micro blogging. Instead of friends, you have followers on Twitter and you follow other people. When you publish content on Twitter it is called a tweet. Your tweets can be a maximum of 280 characters—not words—characters. There is much more rapid-fire activity on Twitter than there is on Facebook, so you need to tweet much more often than you post. Use the hashtag symbol (#) before a keyword in your tweet to help improve engagement with your followers through likes, retweets, and replies. (See the hashtag section in the Appendix for more information on how to use these in your marketing.)

LinkedIn is the professional social media site that focuses on business networking. This is a good outlet for nonfiction authors. When you publish content, it is called a post, and the people you are linked with are called your connections. My posts on LinkedIn are about upcoming conferences where I'm teaching, new book releases, and articles I've published. Think of LinkedIn as the platform to announce what you are doing professionally, in addition to posting content that provides value to your connections.

Similar to having a Facebook author persona, if you already have a LinkedIn profile, you may want another account for your professional author persona. LinkedIn is not a place to post more personal things like you can on Facebook.

Pinterest is like a corkboard filled with images. It is totally visual. The visuals sometimes have words imprinted over the top of them, called memes, like those photographs with a scripture or a quote overlaid. The pictures have links behind them, and you can group these message boards under categories. Use Pic Monkey or some other program to create these memes. Think of Pinterest as a visual Facebook where everything is presented in pictures instead of words.

Instagram is the newest picture child on the block. It is similar to Pinterest, but it has a few features that make it very author-friendly. One thing is the hashtag. Think of hashtags as zip codes for those with like interests. You can create a hashtag for #BeatingFear and #SlayingGiants. Then everyone interested in those topics will be able to find you and follow you.

Making It Happen

There are a lot of social media outlets you can choose from, beyond what is listed in this chapter. You do not have to have accounts for all of them. You have the best chance of success if you start small and build your foundation slowly. I suggest choosing two outlets. Most people choose Facebook and Twitter. However, it all depends on who your target market is. If you're writing for the twenty- to thirty-year-old market, they've left Facebook for Snapchat. Where is your target market hanging out? These are great questions to ask if you survey your readers: What social media are you spending time on? How many times a day are you on social media? Once you've settled on which outlets you're going to start with, it's time to take your list of five content categories and create a social media schedule.

Schedulers

This is the most exciting part of what I'm going to share with you about scheduling social media—free programs. Did I say free? We like free. Picture the dashboard in your car that allows you to see how much gas you have, the temperature of your engine, and all of the gauges for the different things going on in your car. There are several dashboards for your social media including Hootsuite, Kontentino, and Friends+Me. These sites allow you to control your Facebook, Twitter, LinkedIn, Pinterest, and Instagram profiles all in one place.

You can manage one to five platforms for free depending upon which program you choose. Most authors start with Facebook and one other social media account. You might have Twitter, or you might have LinkedIn if your book is more of a professional book. If you have more of a visual-oriented book your second account might be Pinterest or Instagram. Once you have set up your two social media accounts, you will then sign up for one of these scheduler accounts and then connect your social media accounts to the dashboard scheduler. Setting up these accounts involves answering a few questions. It takes some time, but it is very user-friendly.

After you've connected your social media accounts to your dashboard, you're ready to preschedule your social media posts. I use Kontentino and it has set me free. For example, when I speak at conferences I am also posting on Twitter, Facebook, and LinkedIn the entire time. I don't pull out my cell phone or laptop once to do this. I've already scheduled those posts months ahead of time. You will be able to do the same thing using those five content categories you created.

Going back to the Scripture Saturday example, you can schedule posts for the next six Saturdays because you already have your list of scriptures. You can schedule the next six Mondays with your quotes, for Motivational Monday.

When you start writing the content for your social media posts, I recommend you start with your Facebook posts first. Facebook gives you the largest amount of space for content, so you can be a little bit wordier with those posts. After you've finished scheduling your Facebook posts, move on to Twitter if that is your second platform. You only have 280 characters on Twitter, so you will need to condense the content from your Facebook posts that you've already scheduled.

Start by scheduling two weeks of posts to get used to working with your scheduler. After a while it will become second nature. Soon you will notice that you're always on the lookout for new categories and new content to post.

If you come across something interesting for your readers, you can post it right then, schedule it for a future post, or do both. If I find something, I add it to my list to be posted later, but there is certainly nothing wrong with posting something spur-of-the-moment.

A word of caution: be aware of world events. The last thing you want is to appear insensitive because your prescheduled posts don't match the sentiment in the world at the moment. A tragedy in your hometown, a terrorist attack, or a natural disaster should cause you to pray, and then run to your scheduler to remove or change your posts to something more appropriate.

Email Marketing

The key to building your platform is about finding a way to connect with your readers on a consistent, ongoing basis. One of the best ways to do that is through what is known as email marketing or newsletter marketing. When I first started as a speaker, I went to events and book signings and collected business cards. I faithfully brought all of those cards home and put them in a shoebox. I did not have any idea what I was supposed to do with all of those names and addresses and contacts. I just had shoeboxes full of them.

It wasn't until I learned about email marketing that I began to make the connection that all of the people I'm getting business cards from are the people that will form the basis for my email database. You can benefit from my mistake and learn this from the beginning. Rather than collecting business cards and putting them in a shoebox, I suggest that you use a contact collection system like Constant Contact or MailChimp. Both of these are easy-to-use programs for collecting people's names, addresses, and email addresses.

Once you have imported this contact information, these programs then allow you to send out an e-newsletter. There are templates to choose from and you can add your content and images. It's up to you to decide on the frequency of your newsletter. I send mine out quarterly.

In addition to the contacts from the business cards you collect, you can also add contacts by inviting people to sign up for your newsletter through a simple form on your website. Then in your social media posts, every once in a while, mention that you offer a newsletter and that people can subscribe on your website. Remember: the purpose of your social media posts is to drive traffic to your website.

Readers are interested in the newsletters that they've signed up for, and newsletters are another way for you to stay in contact with your readers. If they've signed up for your e-newsletter, they are saying, "Yes, I want more of what you are sharing."

You also want to consider giving something away for free when people sign up for your e-newsletter. You could give an excerpt of your new book that is about to be published, a mini e-booklet that's a free download or PDF, or a prayer calendar. Whatever giveaway you choose, make it something meaningful that is of use to your readers.

Blogs

Many authors have found a blog to be a terrific way of connecting to their readers. On the other hand, there are authors who find it to be one more thing on their endless to-do list that never gets done. So how do you know if a blog is the right marketing tool for you? There are several ways to answer this question. Here are a few things to consider.

A blog is a commitment. If you tell your readers you will blog twice a week, then you need to fulfill that promise. The best blogs are updated at least once each week, but even if you commit to once a month, you need to be consistent.

Do you have something to say? Is it unique in the blogosphere? Begin by doing some research. What are the topics you are most interested in and what do others already say? It doesn't mean you can't write about that topic, you just have to find a unique angle. For instance, perhaps you are a single dad and want to write about parenting girls. You may find several others out there who are doing that, but maybe you are different because you live on a farm. Maybe you are different because you are in the National Guard and must leave for weeks on end. Maybe you homeschool.

Blogs are often a part of your website, but sometimes they are the website. They also can be separate from the website and simply link to it. Which option is best for you is determined by how central your blog content is to your ministry. If most people will know you and connect to you through your blog, then a blog website is best. If your blog is important but not the main reason people connect to you, then it should be a part of your website. If, however, you want to explore several topics that are not closely aligned with the core message of your website, then a separate blog that links to your website is best.

Because a blog speaks to your core messages just like social media does, it is a good practice not to confuse your readers with unrelated content that doesn't support your brand. They won't tell you they're confused, they'll simply leave. Remember when IHOP tried to change to IHOB and their pancake fans threw a fit? They almost lost their loyal customer base because IHOP is for pancakes. IHOP can sell burgers, but they are the International House of Pancakes. Don't make this mistake.

Adding Images

The single best way to generate interest and increase readership for your blog is to include an image with each post. Choose an image that communicates your message, because a lot of people will choose to read or not read your post based upon the image. If the blog post is longer or has more than one key point, break it up with multiple images. You can find images at Google Images, Pexels, Unslpash, and Pixabay.

The next step is to turn some of your images into a meme—an image with a message. Imgflip is a free and easy-to-use tool. I love Canva, but it is a paid service. However, it allows you to create a meme and then resize it for use on all types of social media with just a click of a button. Warning: making memes can become addictive.

Blog Dos and Don'ts

Here are a few things you should do and some you shouldn't if you want to blog:

1. Be consistent. Once a month is better than saying you'll post every day and then not doing it.

2. Add memes. Images break up text, increase interest, and provide a visual representation of your point.

3. Offer links. If you mention resources, a scripture, a quote, or a website, link to it. It helps your reader and it increases Google rankings for your blog.

4. Join hands (or websites). Have a list of linkable blogs on your site for like-minded bloggers. When they reciprocate, your Google rankings will go through the roof—and it is helpful to your readers.

5. Stick to your core messages. Don't confuse your readers, but stick to your core messages to develop your brand and grow your following.

Doing More

At the beginning of the year I look at my overall writing goals, messages, and assignments. I then use my blog posts to double as writing space for what will be used elsewhere. For instance, if I have an article assignment on the Holy Spirit, I plan one of my blogs to be on that topic so my research and writing can be reused for the article.

Amazon Author Page

One of things that amazes me is the number of authors on Amazon who have not taken advantage of this free service. When an author has a book on Amazon, if their name is hyperlinked you can click on it and go to their author page to learn more about them. This simple step increases book sales. It not only proves your legitimacy as an author, but it gives you certain functions and capabilities on Amazon that will help to convert readers into fans. An Amazon Author Page is where people can learn more about you, see (and buy) all your books, and find your website, blog, or social media all in one spot. Here are the steps:

1. Go to authorcentral.amazon.com and click Join Now.

2. Sign in with your Amazon account information.

3. Enter the name of your book and choose one to create your account.

4. A confirmation email will be sent to you to finish your setup.

You will need the following to create a fully functional author page:

1. A well-written author bio in third person (Read other bios to get a feel for what works best.)

2. A great headshot

3. Links to all of your books on Amazon

4. Book trailers or YouTube videos

5. A link to your blog feed (Make sure you enter the feed address and not simply your blog address.)

6. A link to your website

7. Links to your social media accounts

After you create a beautiful Amazon Author Page, the final step is to change the URL or the link of your page to one that doesn't scream immature. Here are the steps:

1. On the Profile tab, click add link next to "Author Page URL."

2. A recommended URL will appear, but you can choose your own.

3. If the URL you typed is available, click save.

Now that you have your own unique Amazon Page URL, you can add it to your author email signature, your website, or your social media.

Ministry in Action–Cheri Cowell

EABooks Publishing specializes in helping the technically challenged, and one of our authors was just that. She was in her eighties and hired us to publish her memoir about her years in the mission field. After her book was published, she called me in a panic. She explained that she didn't understand anything we were telling her to do in a recent email we'd sent her.

After I calmed the author down, I asked her to explain. She said she didn't understand the first sentence of the email where it said she has a URL — she didn't know what that was (a URL is a website address). I smiled. Then I said to her, "Didn't you say you have a grandson who lives nearby?" She said she did.

"I want you to call your grandson to come over, and then show him that URL and tell him you want to send an email to all of your friends with that in it, okay?" She said she could do that, and I told her to ignore everything else in the email.

Two weeks later, the author's missionary book was on Amazon's top 100 list in her category. She did not use all of the social media and marketing techniques we are teaching in this book. She didn't know what a URL was, but she took steps of faith and God blessed it.

Do I know how this happened? No, I really don't. I could point to many authors who've done everything right. They've built a solid foundation to market their book, created their author platform, ministered to their readers' needs, and their books have never been on Amazon's lists. I can also point to many who, like this author, don't do these things and God blesses their efforts. All I can encourage you to do is, do what you can with the time, energy, and resources you have, and do it with the right heart. God will bless your efforts — maybe with an Amazon top 100 ranking, but maybe not. We do the work and leave the results up to God.

Chapter 4

The Best Time to Start Marketing

Authors often ask me, when is the best time to start marketing their book. The answer surprises many of them — the best time is actually before the book is finished. If you've already written your book you can still go back and do this work, but I encourage you to begin your marketing efforts while you are still writing.

The Most Important Decision

When authors are asked to describe his or her target audience, a common response is, "There is something for everyone in my book." While they may truly believe that, it is just not possible to target "everyone." Some authors are afraid that if they focus on a more narrow audience they will lose out on book sales. What you will find is that the opposite is true.

Getting specific about your audience will help you build that solid foundation for all of your marketing efforts. It will help you identify your core messages and write the content

47

for your website, your social media posts, and your articles. It will help you decide which marketing efforts are worth your time, and which ones waste your time. To successfully market your book, you need to define your target audience in detail, and in doing so you will gain sales. Here is an exercise that will help you do that.

First, find a magazine with pictures of people in it and choose a picture of someone who represents the person you are writing your book to. Cut out the picture and glue or tape it to a piece of blank paper. Next to the picture, I want you to describe this person. What is this person like? What is their personality? Are they married? Do they have kids? Describe what their day is like. What time do they wake up? Are they rushing off to work? Are they grabbing a bagel? Are they going to Starbucks? Are they getting kids ready for school? Packing school lunches? Do they work outside the home? Are they a carpool mom?

Next, begin to describe this person's spiritual well-being. Do they begin their day with prayer? Are they too rushed to think about that? Are they involved in a Bible study at church? Do they even go to church? Where would they go to get their faith questions answered? Are they Googling their faith questions? Or do they have a neighbor or a friend who is exemplifying what a Christian life is and they're curious? Do they attend church and maybe have a quasi-relationship with God? Or are they super-busy at church, involved in every single activity there, and exhausted because they are the "yes" person at church?

Then describe what their evening is like. How do they wrap up their day? Are they rushing through carpool lines? Are they running home from work? Did they finish their day at five and now have to pick their kids up at day care and get dinner on the table? Do they feel mom guilt because their kids are in after-school programs?

This exercise is basically a character analysis on your reader. This is a familiar concept for those of you who are fiction writers. When you get to the end of this process you will have someone specific you are writing your book for.

When I write my books, I do this exercise and tape that piece of paper on my computer screen so that I am writing directly to that person. This exercise will help you focus everything in your writing process, and your marketing. If what you are writing does not address that reader and that reader's issues, it does not belong in your book. Don't sway from your purpose.

New writers typically think they have more than one reader. Wrong answer. You need to be writing to one person as though it is a personal communication between you and your reader. Get to know that reader so well that you want to help them. Become intimate with that reader.

Yes, people other than that one person will read your book. The purpose of this exercise is to train your mind to zero in on that one person. In doing so, your writing and your marketing will become crisp and focused.

While You Are Still Writing

You will find many ways to market directly to this person as you're writing. You will collect all kinds of research and information that will not fit directly into your book, but it can still be useful. The extra material will work well for ministering to this person. It will be the basis for all of your marketing efforts. In fact, I love it when someone comes to us at EABooks Publishing with more information than they know what to do with. We are able to use all of that extra information, and you can, too. Here are some ideas for that.

Teasing

As you're writing your book, you want to build a fan base that is interested in your book. Invite readers into your world. Share what's going on. You do this by giving tidbits through your social media outlets and on your blog: "I was doing some research today, and I ran across this quote . . . " or, "I ran across this bit of research, and I was so floored. How many of you know about such and such?" Then you share what it is you have.

Here's an idea for fiction specifically. I'm working on a book that is set in the 1840s. I researched transportation in the 1840s because my character travels when the railroad was being built. I learned about the bunkhouses that were created during this time. I tweeted and posted on Facebook about what I'm learning, and now there are readers who say they want the book as soon as it's available. They want it because they found the information I posted to be interesting. So your research can become teasers for your upcoming book.

People are also interested in how you're writing your book. It's something many people dream of doing, but few actually do it. Share those parts of your journey as an author and they will feel that they are partners with you in writing your book. This is true especially if you ask for feedback. Ask questions like, "What do you think about this name for a character versus this name?" This builds a connection with your readers, and they become vested in you getting your book published. When your book is released, they will want to buy a copy because they've been with you on your writing journey.

Research Reused

When you are writing, you gather a lot of research. If you are writing historical fiction, you research the type of clothing that was in style, what food people ate, and the customs for the time period. Not all of this information will make it into your book, but it still serves a purpose. It is great content for blog posts, articles, tweets, and other social media posts. You can use your research, especially in nonfiction, as content for tip sheets and other free downloads from your website.

For those of you who are writing fiction or a memoir, you can talk about the research material you found for the time period that you are writing in. Maybe you learned about fashion or table etiquette. There are all kinds of topics you researched that would be interesting for your readers. You could write articles or blog posts using some of the meditative prayers from the time period your book is written in. Maybe they said a special grace during that time that people would love to use today.

I was amazed to discover I had quotable phrases in my book that I could reuse for social media posts. We don't think of our book that way when we're writing it. We're just writing it and hoping that every once in a while we've crafted a wonderful sentence. But all of that writing can be reused. So, sit with your book and a yellow highlighter while you're watching TV and go through it with different eyes—look at it as a source for tweets and posts.

Articles

This is one of my favorite tips. A book is simply a series of articles strung together under like categories—

chapter headings. Submit articles using the material for your book; then take all the articles and make transitions between them to create chapters.

This is the best way to write a book, especially nonfiction. Start writing articles, do the work to get them published, and then collect all of the articles and assemble your book. This is a simple concept, but it is going to require some finesse. You will need to learn how to transition, because not all articles flow smoothly from one chapter to the next. But you will see that a chapter in a book is basically an article. How fun is that?

Ancillary Products

Your research material can also be used to help you come up with ideas for ancillary products. There are all kinds of products that you can sell either from your website or when you are speaking. These are great ways to remind people of your talk, your book, and the take-away messages you hope to impart. Go to an online printer and look at their products section for ideas. You can create calendars, quote books, or jewelry. There are so many different things that you could do. For instance, my first book, *Direction, Discernment for the Decisions of*

Your Life, had an apple and orange on the front cover. I had some jewelry made up with tiny apples and oranges, and then I created a scripture card that went with the jewelry.

Speaking

I'm not going to go into too much detail here on speaking, but you do *not* want to speak on your book. It sounds like a sales pitch, and nobody wants to sit there and have somebody read from his or her book. That is boring, so don't do it.

Instead, think about what you could do to teach about one of the core messages or themes in your book. For example, one of the chapters in my *Direction* book is about hearing from God in a noisy world. I took that chapter and created an entire conference about listening to God in a noisy world. It's not my book. It is a chapter in my book. See how this works?

I don't promote my book. I share something meaningful and helpful to people, and then hopefully they will want to buy my book because I've ministered to them.

Topics for speaking on fiction can come from all of your research. You might think it is something everyone knows already, but they really don't. They don't know how a writer's life works. They don't understand how you come up with your topics. They don't understand how you would create that fantasy world. People are fascinated by all of those things. You think it's old hat because it's where you live. However, your audience is interested in that, so you could put together a whole presentation on creating a fantasy world. Then you could end with a take-away nugget—such as we all want to escape to a fantasy world, but we need to live in reality. They will love you because you haven't delivered a preachy message. You've given them something that will make them say, "Wow. That was interesting. That was good. I'm going to go buy that book." Because you've made a friend, right? And friends buy friends' books. That's what we're after.

Ministry in Action–Michelle Booth, Marketing Coach

During an introductory marketing coaching call with a new author, we were discussing big-picture issues: Why did you write your book? Who did you write your book for? What is your goal for your book? At one point during our conversation, the author made the comment that it was probably too early to start telling people she was publishing a book, since her manuscript was still in editing. She was surprised when I told her it was definitely not too early.

I encouraged her to start promoting her book right away, and as often as she could. I explained that she did not need a final manuscript, book cover design, marketing campaign, and book launch in place before she could begin marketing her book. Then we got busy brainstorming all of the things she could do in advance of her publishing date.

Over the next several months, as the author's manuscript was being edited, we did the work to set up her social media accounts, start building her email database, and plan the content for her upcoming social media posts and newsletters. She began posting on her author Facebook page right away and writing content for her quarterly newsletters.

The author had an existing website that we were helping her redesign. While we were working on this behind the scenes, she continued writing blog posts that she uploaded to her existing site. She didn't focus on asking people to buy her book in her posts. Instead, her content was about the themes in her book and the messages she had for her readers.

She started spreading the word about her book whenever she spoke at meetings. Her book wasn't the main topic of her speech, but she would briefly refer to her book at some point during her presentation. She was pleasantly surprised as she did. People would often approach her after the meetings and ask to be updated on her publishing date so they could be sure to buy a copy of her book when it came out. That gave her the opportunity to collect more email addresses and continue building her contact database.

The author began reaching out to organizations to schedule herself as a speaker once her book was published. She found they were receptive to her pitch even though she didn't have a published book in hand. She also took excerpts from her book and turned them into articles that she pitched to different publications.

By being authentic and engaging with her audience well in advance of her publishing date, the author was able to build awareness and anticipation about her book. This was all done while she was moving her manuscript from editing into publishing.

Blueprint for Action

As authors, we often want to know what to *do*, when in actuality the best thing we can do is to *think* correctly. If our thinking is right, then our actions will follow, and it won't be such hard work. So, what are we thinking? I've mentioned this several times now — you need to think differently and put on different hats throughout the process of publishing a book. In this section, I am going to invite you to think in different ways about investments you need to make while working on your book.

Think Marketing

As you are writing, consider the investment of hiring a publicist or a marketing coach — someone to come alongside of you and help you in this process.

A publicist will be able to help with one part of a marketing plan. For instance, you could hire a publicist to arrange a blog tour for you. A publicist can schedule radio interviews, television interviews, or get newspaper, magazine, and online article assignments.

A marketing coach is a broader term. This is someone who will look at the big picture and help you determine what marketing strategies you need, which could include publicity.

Think Proposal

Some independent publishers, like EABooks, don't require a book proposal. This is good news to a lot of people because they don't want to write one. However, you probably should do it anyway. The information included in a proposal is important for you to know, whether you are traditionally publishing or independently publishing.

The proposal is your sales material that you will use to pitch your book to a publishing house. But more than that, everything you have to create for a book proposal is going to help you focus your writing and your marketing. You need to know who your competitors are and what makes you unique and different in the market. You need to know your hook, your target market, and your core message. Invest time in gathering this information.

Your Hook

If you go to a writers' conference, you are going to hear the phrase "the hook" over and over again. The best definition that I've heard for the hook is this: it is the one sentence that best describes how you and your book meet the needs of your reader. It takes enormous amounts of thought to create this one sentence because it has to be succinct. It has to be so well targeted that you will need to spend a lot of time working on this single sentence.

Identifying your hook is another way to help focus your writing project. The reason why the hook is the first item in a book proposal is because it is so important. It tells the publisher, it tells the reader, and it tells you as the author why your book was written.

An exercise to help you identify your hook is to invest time in writing your back-cover copy. It's hard to craft those five or six sentences that go on the back of a book. Whether or not this becomes the actual back-cover copy doesn't matter. Creating it will help you write your book and stay true to your message.

Go to your local Christian bookstore and spend time reading the back-cover copy of books that are similar to yours. Once you've done this, you will be ready to craft your own back-cover copy. That is your hook; the essence of your book is in that back-cover copy.

Think Editing

My first recommendation to some of our authors is to send their book to one of our editors. Editing is an investment in future sales. A well-edited manuscript is going to sell better than a book that is poorly edited. You can have a beautifully designed cover, back-cover copy that is well-written, and a professional website, but if the content of your book is lacking—if it doesn't flow, if it is written in passive voice, if the sentence structure is awkward, if there are mechanical errors—your book will not sell.

Keep in mind that editing can be expensive. A professional editor—not your friend or someone you know who likes to read—is worthy of their pay. You can spend anywhere from five hundred dollars to three thousand dollars on a good edit, depending upon your word count and what kind of editing you need—developmental, content, or line editing—and how many rounds of editing you need. This is where authors tend to want to skimp because they don't understand that investing in editing is necessary for future sales. Even now, I pay an outside editor to edit my manuscript before I send it to the traditional publisher, who will also edit it.

Think Shopping

Invest some time thinking about where your reader shops for books and how they get their questions answered. Go back to the picture that you cut out and the character analysis you did on your target reader. Remember what their day is like. What do they Google? What groups are they a part of? Where do they hang out on the weekend? What social media are they a part of? How are you going to reach that person?

Here are some more investments to consider for your blueprint for action.

Survey

Conducting a survey is a fruitful effort you can invest in. Surveys are great if your target market is your tribe. You need an established connection with a group of people in order to send out a survey, otherwise it won't work. I like Survey Monkey, but there are several other free survey applications available. You can also post questions on Facebook.

A survey is how I found out that my target market uses e-readers. This blew my mind. In my survey, I asked about my target market's reading habits. Where do they go to shop for their books? Are they more likely to buy a print book or an e-book? Where would they buy that? Do they go to the Christian bookstore or do they go to a Barnes & Noble? Would they prefer to shop at a bookstore or on Amazon?

I found out that my readers are like 85 percent of the people out there: they shop on Amazon. They might go into the bookstore and look at the book, but then they order it from Amazon. I go in and I feel the book, I smell it, I get so excited, and I buy the book. But that's not what my target audiences does. Surveying my readers was a real eye-opener.

Bookstore

Invest in visiting a bookstore with your marketing hat on—not your author hat—for the purpose of research. Look for books like yours and see who is writing the endorsements. Look for trends with book covers. It used to be that there were lots of paths (literally) on book covers: wooded paths, brick paths, and roads. People seem to be the trend right now— backs and side views of people. You need to know what the cover trend is for books in your genre.

If you're writing nonfiction, you need to know what the hot topics are right now. If you are independently publishing, you can jump on those hot topics because our publishing process is only ninety days. If you are going the traditional route, it's a one- to two-year process, so you need to consider whether or not that trend will still exist then.

We tend not to go to the magazine section because we're book people, but the magazine section is your trendsetter. Look at the topics that are being covered beyond the evergreen topics. Yes, every magazine in January is about fitness and diet, but there are other articles besides those, so look at the trends. See what's being discussed. See what questions are being answered. Magazines can give you insight into where the world is right now.

Google Keywords

Invest some time Googling the search terms you think your target market is going to use to look for answers to their questions on the topic you're writing about. Pay attention to what results come up. What answers are your readers getting for the questions they're asking? Find out what they're being told. That will be eye-opening, especially if you write on controversial topics. They're being given a lot of information we don't agree with, but you need to know that. Essentially, what you're doing here is looking at what your competition is telling your readers. This will give you insight into how you are different, and how your answers to their questions are going to meet their needs versus what they're being told by others.

Your Competition

Invest in learning about your competition. This is a combination of searching Google and visiting the bookstore. You need to know where the answers to your readers' questions are coming from. This may take you into uncomfortable territory, but you need to go there. Maybe there are chat rooms you can hang out in. Pray yourself up before you go into some of these places. You need to know why you're there, and you need to know that you are covered in the blood of Jesus. You are good. You are safe. But you need to go there so you can hear what your readers are being told, the answers they're being given, and how persuasive those answers are. You need to know how truly lost these people are who are looking for answers, and how they are begging for someone to give them the truth. They know in their spirits, inside of their hearts, that they're not getting the truth, yet, and that's why they're still searching.

You don't know what you're going to find when you research your competition. God might open doors for you that you had no idea He was going to open because He needs someone in that dark place to speak truth. Listen to what God might want to do with you while you're there.

Think about Your Strengths and Weaknesses

What are your strengths? Some of us are gifted at storytelling, but we're not as gifted at marketing. You can learn different skills, but there comes a time when it's better to hire someone than it is to spend time learning to overcome your particular area of weakness.

I've learned that I am good at writing content for my social media posts, but I'm not so good at the technical side of social media. Knowing this, I hired a social media manager to take everything I write and schedule my posts. This is partly because I run a company, but I also do many other things and I'm trying to keep my head above water. The other part of it is — it's just not my strength. My social media manager is a stay-at-home mom. By scheduling my posts, she earns some money and is also able to be with her kids. So I'm blessing somebody else, I'm blessing me, and I am spending my time where my strengths are.

Think Giving

We are writers and we want to sell our books and articles and make some money. That is important, but we also need to think about what we can give to our readers. What can you give away to bless someone, help someone, or thank someone?

Many authors struggle with this because they are afraid if they give things away then people won't want to buy their book. All I can tell you is the more you give, truly, the more you receive. This biblical principle is something that the whole world operates on, and it applies to marketing your book as well.

Think about what can do with all of the material and knowledge you've gained in writing your books and articles. You can give away resources, puzzles, or coloring sheets. You can take parts of your book and expound on them.

In my *Direction* book, I have a chapter on hearing from God. There is more that I can say on that topic than there was room for in the book. I don't want to repeat everything that's in the book in my marketing, but I can add to it. I can give top-five prayer tips. I can give the best scriptures to use for contemplative prayer. I can give scripture references that are good if you are seeking wisdom. I can talk about the different methods for having a prayer time when leading a small group. This could be a tip sheet or a suggestion sheet that would be great for small-group leaders on leading circle prayers or forgiveness prayers.

Spend time thinking about each part of your book and what content your readers might be interested in that you can give away. I promise you, you cannot out-give God.

Think about Your Time

Most of us are trained that time is something we can continually give and it doesn't cost us anything. But if you look at your writing from a business perspective — as you should — you need to attach a dollar figure to your time.

For instance, when I started getting really busy writing articles, writing my next book, and marketing my book, there came a time when I had to decide if my time was better spent writing that next article or cleaning my house. I realized at that point that it was a good investment for me to pay someone to clean my house so I could spend my time on what was going to get me to the next stage in my writing career.

The question is, what is your time worth? It is going to be a different trade-off for everyone. At different stages in your writing career, you will have to decide what things are worth paying for so you can focus on the things that only you can do. That is what makes EABooks Publishing a perfect fit for some people. They've decided it is worth it to pay us to do the things that they don't have time to do.

One of our authors who is also an artist had to decide whether it was a better use of her time to learn how to use Photoshop and InDesign so she could design her book cover, or to have one of our designers create her cover. You can learn how to format your book, design your book cover, and create your website. The question is whether you should be spending your time doing those things or writing your next book.

Think Soft-Sell

All of us have seen authors on Facebook and Twitter who only talk about their book, their reviews, their speaking engagements, and themselves. This self-promotion gives book marketing a bad reputation. There is another way to promote your book that involves talking about the message God has given you rather than about your book.

In the soft-sell approach, your book is the vehicle you will use to communicate your message to your readers. Think about marketing as ministry. Don't talk about the book in your marketing, talk about the message.

In my book *Living the Story*, I talk about connecting with the gospel in a way that meets people where they are. When I'm talking to people, I say, "Do you have family or friends you would like to share the gospel with, but who have put up walls? People who don't want to hear about your faith, but are looking for answers to their life's problems? They are looking for peace. They are looking for joy. They are looking for a friend who understands their pain and suffering. They're looking for someone who will never let them down."

Do you hear the difference in that approach? I talk about something that meets them where they are. I'm also sharing that the book I've published has a story thread throughout it that discusses what living that life looks like to the world and how you can demonstrate that.

I don't say, "In my book . . ." Instead, I allow my radio interviewer or the byline at the bottom of the article to speak that message for me. My role is to share the message.

The number one question about this approach that I hear from authors is, "Why would people want to buy my book if I share all of the information that's in the book?" You will be amazed how well this soft-sell approach works. It's actually biblical. Jesus did the very same thing. He told parables, and those stories always pointed to His heavenly Father. Jesus Himself was the answer, just like your book is the answer. But you don't say, "In my book," and Jesus didn't say, "The answer is in my Father." He let His stories reveal the answer and point directly to His Father.

You will do the same thing when you share an article. In your byline you will point to your book. In my bio underneath an article where I've shared information, it says, "Cheri Cowell is the author of *Living the Story* where she shares examples of how it would look if you were to truly be the story that people need to read." People will read that bio and say, "Oh, that sounds like the book that I've been looking for." They will click on the link and buy the book because I've spoken about the truth in the book. By using the soft-sell approach you're allowing your message to do the selling for you. That is marketing as ministry.

Chapter 5

Icing the Cake

In today's publishing world, you must have an online presence. By that I don't mean just your website. When someone searches your name, pages of content need to come up in the results. When you plug in Cheri Cowell, you will probably get eight pages of content. I work hard to maintain that, and the way to do that is by writing good content that can be used on multiple sites. Most of these sites are not going to pay, but you need to think of your pay being that higher ranking on Google. When somebody plugs in your name and eight pages come up, they are thinking, "Wow, there's a lot of information here. I need to learn about this person."

Evergreen Articles

To maintain an online presence, I suggest using a six-month calendar to help you plan. Start filling in your calendar with topics for evergreen articles—those articles that come up every year in specific months. January magazines talk about exercise because we've eaten a lot over the previous months and now we all have a goal of losing weight. There are articles on healthy eating, New Year's resolutions, and how to get out of debt because we've spent a lot of money over the holidays. February is the love month. It does not have to be romantic love. It can be love of those who are difficult to love, love between you and God, or how to love yourself. Sometimes March is the month of Easter, but March is also about spring. Look at each month of the year. Think about the magazines and then think about your book. How would you tie those together?

In January I talk about using wisdom to set goals, exercising your spiritual muscles, and good prayer exercises. I talk about losing weight—what things you need to eliminate from your life that are preventing you from good spiritual practices. Maybe there are some people in your life who are difficult and are always dragging you down. Maybe it's best to replace some of those friends. There are all sorts of topics I am talking about in January. Every year I am writing those articles and tying my book *Direction* to those magazines.

Where do you publish these articles online? This is where all of that research you did for your keyword search comes in. The websites that came up in the searches you did are websites that are looking for good content.

I also want to make sure you are aware of the *The Christian Writer's Market Guide*. A new edition of this book is published every year. It includes every outlet that is looking for freelance authors. It tells you everything you need to know about submitting online and print articles. I suggest you get that book. Look for your keywords and you will find a list of the periodicals and magazines that are looking for your content.

Don't dismiss some of the often-overlooked opportunities to get published. In the Appendix is a list of some of my favorites. Not all of these will lend themselves to topics from your book, but all of them offer bylines, and those bylines can link back to your website, increasing your web presence and your Google rankings. It is all good.

Once you have created your list of topics and outlets and categorized them by month, you are ready to create your six-month or one-year online presence plan.

Book Launch Plan

The first thing authors usually want to talk about when they are publishing a book is their book launch. They envision an author-signing event with long lines of people eager to buy their book. That is one part of a book launch, but it is not the only part.

When we talk about a launch plan at EABooks, we focus on what will help build excitement around the time your book is published. Think of your book launch as a two-week period to toot your own horn and invite people to buy your book (after those two weeks, you will shift your focus to the other marketing efforts we've been discussing in this book).

Family, friends, and everyone you meet understand that publishing a book is exciting and they want to help you celebrate. How do you make the most out of this goodwill? Begin by collecting as many pre-orders as you can. Specify that you want people to buy your book during this two-week window—either from you or by using a link that you will send them.

With a free program called Rafflecopter, you can design a promotion so that when people buy a book on your website, their name will be entered into a drawing for a giveaway. Make it something people really want . . . perhaps a basket of books!

Ministry in Action–Laurie Copeland, Marketing Coach

Art—more than almost anything else—has emotional attachments. You are attached to your writing; your entire publication time period has probably felt like you birthed a baby, and now you await the reviews. A good review could send you soaring into the clouds; a bad review may put you in the dumps. It's emotional. It's also emotional for your audience. Have you ever just met someone where there's an instant attachment—you just know you could be friends? This is how it feels for your audience to love your art—writing, in your case.

So this is where you start when it comes to your launch. We use your art as a means to an end:

- Like a behind-the-scenes video, tell the creation story of how your work came to be. Use your mailing list or social media to tell this story.

- Tell your audience what you are doing for your work: research, travel, rest, play-time, writing habits. Because you are an artist, followers assume what you are doing is cool—you may not agree, but they think it is.

- Engage your tribe. Give away something or ask for their opinions, thereby building ownership. Make people feel connected and they'll get behind you.

What you are doing even before the launch party happens is building your community by letting them get to know you and your work, thereby building anticipation for your launch.

- Example 1: One of my authors has written a book and journal/planner that combines all our areas of life within a spiritual framework that will produce a life of true fulfillment. She is currently testing her method and running through the entire seven weeks with two small groups, working out the kinks before she launches it to the public. She is building her community well before the launch even happens.

- Example 2: One client is a speaker and author whose audience is family members of addicts, and are without hope. She beautifully plays the behind-the-scenes video of her life by sharing her own story and struggle with her son's addiction and the life-giving hope she received through verses in the book of Jeremiah.

- Example 3: Another author has written a devotional and has a Facebook prayer group (her social media community) that meets weekly via Facebook for prayer. This is her avenue for staying in touch with her community's needs. Her audience feels like they know her because her devotionals reflect stories from her own life. Before her launch party, she ordered postcards, business cards, and made a poster, then posted an invitation on Facebook and sent one to everyone on her Christmas card list. When her books arrived, she posted on Facebook a picture of her books still in the box. She advertised on a local radio station. All those "little" things she did, added up—her books sold out at the launch party! She continues her sales online, and her community thrives with her Facebook prayer group.

A Team Approach

A team is better than one, and a book launch team, or a street team as they are often called, is vital for a successful book launch. These are people who believe in you and your message. Add people to your team who are great with different social media outlets, some who will love to help set up and run your book-signing event, and others who are great at word-of-mouth advertising. Then arm your team with the tools to help you. Here is a list of what they will need.

1. Access to you. They need to know you will answer their texts and emails right away. Set them up on a group email and group text. Set up a conference call several months in advance so they can get excited together and share what they are doing—excitement is contagious.

2. The memes you create. They need one meme to announce they are part of your team, a general heads-up meme, and then a new meme for every day of the two-week launch.

3. Email announcements. Create announcements they can send that include links to your website, ordering page, and Amazon.

4. Content for social media. Write the posts and tweets in advance so they can simply cut and paste.

5. A reward/incentive. Create a contest for your street team to help keep them motivated. The prize is an MVP Award that goes to the person who outdoes him or herself in promotion. Make the competition fun and lighthearted.

Finally, during your two-week book launch window, I encourage you not only to focus on yourself and your team, but to spend some time in prayer. Begin praying ahead of time that everyone who receives your book during those two weeks will be given a blessing. Invite your team to join you in these prayers. You will be amazed what will happen when you bathe your book launch in prayer, because God really does want to use your book as a tool for His Kingdom and His glory.

Book Signing Event

Notice I chose the word "event," because the statistics are not very favorable for the typical author signing—most people sell fewer than five books. An event is the way to turn that statistic around.

What do I mean by event? This goes back to our marketing philosophy—it is not about you or your book. Even though it is an Author Release or Author Signing, it needs to be so much more. There are many engaging ways to have a book signing without sitting at a bookstore and waiting for people to walk in the door.

As an incentive to bring people to the event, consider hosting a drawing or tying in to some other special event if your book is connected to a cause. We worked with an author whose children's book was about a rescued golden retriever, so her book launch event supported a golden retriever rescue charity. Another author wrote a fiction book about sex trafficking. She hosted a community awareness event in conjunction with her book signing. She teamed up with a ministry that rescues girls from sex trafficking and that does free fingerprinting of children to assist police in finding them if they are lost or kidnapped.

Think outside the box when choosing a venue for your event. If your book has a garden in it, contact your local garden club or a nursery about having an event there. The golden retriever book-signing event was held outside of a PetSmart. What venue might lend itself well to your event because of the themes within your book? You can come up with many different tie-ins by thinking creatively.

If you have an author-signing event, encourage your family and friends to buy the book at the event, not online. As you are planning your book launch, make sure your social media posts focus on building excitement for the event. Offer giveaways that are tied to your book—either for free or in exchange for their email address. You could also offer a gift with purchase.

Online Parties/Launches

Many authors today are finding great success with online launch parties or book parties. Visit virtual book launches around the web and work out what you like, what you don't like, and how you can make yours better. Simply type "Virtual Book Launch" into your search bar or on Facebook, and pick from the dozens of launches that are happening every week—join, participate, or just observe.

Determine when you'd like to host your event. You can do it on launch day or tie it in to something else that is happening. Maybe your book is about Martin Luther King, Jr. His birthday would be a perfect day for a party. Next, decide how long your party will be. Having it last all day will capture all time zones, but it will be a turnoff for those who want to be there for all of the action.

Finally, decide which platform works best for you. Some like the ease of a Facebook Event (choose Create Event in the left-hand column on your page), and others enjoy Facebook Live for those with a professional Facebook page. Google "Set up a Live Video Broadcast" for step-by-step instructions.

Here are some more things to consider when creating your virtual launch party.

1. Create an attractive Facebook banner for your event.

2. Invite strategically. Of course, invite family and friends, but think bigger. Invite influencers,

bloggers, fellow authors in your genre, and online content editors.

3. Share the link for the event on your social media and invite your launch team to do so, too.

4. Create a schedule. Plan an agenda of guest interviews, questions, games, giveaways, and contests.

5. Prepare answers in advance to as many questions you can think of, because during the event you won't be able to write, listen, and interact all at once.

6. Express your gratitude. A launch is not just about you. Remember to thank those who contributed to your success, tell stories, and offer gifts — signed autograph copies are great, but must be mailed. So think about what you could create that you can email — a poem, scripture cards, tip sheets.

7. Ask. People want to be asked to participate, so ask them to buy books during the party, ask them to post a review, or ask them to publish a Facebook post with a link to your website or your book. Invite them to take a picture of themselves reading your

book and offer to enter their names in a drawing. Have fun with the ask.

Online Book Tours

Sometimes referred to as blog tours, online book tours are becoming a must-have in an author's book launch plan. Here are the basic steps to make the blog tour a reality for your next book release.

1. An online book tour takes time and effort, so begin four to six months in advance by compiling a list of bloggers who might be interested in your book—this can be for a book review, a question and answer segment, an excerpt, a book giveaway, a guest post, or a combination of these. Not all blogs will be a good fit, so do your research.

2. Create a spreadsheet for collecting information from these sites. What do they do, what do they require, what are their deadlines, and what is their contact information?

3. Next, determine your "tour date." Perhaps one of these sites only has an opening during a particular week, so allow that to determine your tour date. Maybe your publisher has a big promotional push

planned for a particular week and you want to take advantage of that. Two weeks is a good time frame to aim for, but realize not everyone will "fit" into your plan. Some of these stops on your blog tour will be outliers, and that's okay.

4. Create your media kit, which will include a jpeg of your book cover, short and long book description, author bio and jpeg headshot, and author Q&A. Some blogs will have their own list of questions, but some will use yours. When you are doing your research in step one, note what kinds of questions are asked so you can include those in your list.

5. Next, craft your pitch email to each blog site, telling a little about your book and why you think it would be of interest to the readers on that blog. Do not send a generic pitch to every blogger. Tailor each pitch for the specific audience you want to address. Mention the week you're available and then offer to extend that to another week if the first week doesn't work for them. In your spreadsheet, keep track of what you are sending and the responses you receive.

6. Two weeks prior to your blog tour, recruit a few fans to help you promote it by mentioning your online book tour on their own blogs, Facebook, Twitter, and Pinterest pages. Provide these fans with ready-made memes, posts, and email messages so they can copy and paste them easily.

7. During the blog tour, be sure you are commenting and responding on the blog sites where you are being hosted. Remember, the idea is to engage with your readers.

8. Be sure to send the free books/downloads to the winners of the drawings on the tour within a timely manner. Always remember to send thank-you notes to the blog hosts.

9. Finally, don't judge your tour's success by your Amazon rankings. Your tour will be successful if you connected to a reader, made a new fan, or blessed your tour host by being a great guest. Book sales will follow — maybe not for months down the road. However you and I count our success, online book tours are simply one more tool, one more way, for us to get the word out.

Online Book Clubs

BookBub is a free online service that helps authors get their books in front of readers. It is the 2,230th most visited website in the United States and the biggest and most successful book promotion site in the world for publishers and authors. Millions of email subscribers have signed up to learn more about books like yours, and an author profile on BookBub is free!

Creating an author profile on BookBub is a great marketing tool because it not only gets you more exposure, but readers can also follow you on the site and get notified whenever you release a new book. It's like having an extra promotional email list just for your most dedicated fans on BookBub. And most importantly, you can link directly from your author profile on BookBub to your website. Getting a link from such a popular website can provide a huge Search Engine Optimization (SEO) boost to your website, meaning you'll be getting more web traffic and visitors through Google and other search engines.

Goodreads is another popular online book club. This site allows readers to list the books they've read, and give those books a star rating and an optional review. Then as they connect to friends with the same reading interests, they can see the books their friends have read and the ratings for those books. As an author, you can tap into this word-of-mouth advertising for free. The author program allows published authors to claim their profile page to promote their book and engage with readers. Once verified, your author profile will include the official Goodreads Author badge, which you can use to invite your fans to follow you on Goodreads. You can ask fans to add your book to Listopia, do a book giveaway, or host an Author Q&A, all on Goodreads.

Traditional Book Tours

Most non-authors still believe that publishers send their authors on book tours around the country. But the truth is, that only happens for a very few. The rest of us must plan and fund our own tours. If you've always dreamed of going on a book tour, you can do it yourself. I did.

I joined hands with an author friend and we got out a big map and circled all of the places where we had friends or family. We sent emails to them asking if they'd be willing to take our publicity packet to their women's ministry director or pastor and host us for a night in their home.

We mapped out our tour that covered three states based upon where we had an event and a place to stay. We filled in the gaps in our tour by contacting libraries, schools, and bookstores along the way where we could do an author event. We spent two weeks on the road, sold books, and made new friends. I'm not sure we made a ton of money, but it was fun. It was also a lot of work, so make sure this is something you will enjoy. The memories we made are priceless.

Media Tours

Radio and television interviews are the dream of many authors. As with most opportunities, it is a good idea to do your research first. Identify which shows are the best fit for reaching your target audience. When you craft your pitch, keep in mind that the media can't interview your book, and the fact that you have published a new book is not newsworthy. Explain what topic you will be addressing, why it's important to their audience, and why you are the best person to be interviewed. A generic pitch to a broad list of media contacts is a waste of your time and theirs. You need to customize your pitch for each outlet you are approaching.

To prepare for the actual interview, watch the television shows you want to be interviewed on. What is the style of the interview? Is the author in control or is the interviewer?

Watch how the more skilled authors redirect questions back to their main points. Also note how some authors openly point to their book, while others more subtly generate interest in their book by drawing listeners in.

Now that you've done your research, create a series of questions that mirror those you hear, and then practice your answers. For television, practice in front of your phone or computer by doing a video recording. Practice until you look and feel comfortable. For radio, record yourself and take note of the throat clearing, the ummms, and repeated phrases. Continue practicing until you hear very few of these.

Finally, if this is going to be a big part of your marketing plan, take a class at conferences to learn good interview techniques, and to practice your stage presence. Radio is often an easier entry into the land of interviewing. Begin with your local radio stations and then branch out from there.

Newspapers

Yes, the number of printed newspapers is declining, but many local papers still offer great opportunities for authors. Your hometown news will be interested in the "local kid turned author." Your college paper and newsletters or clubs and organizations you belong to may be good avenues for a local story. These papers don't have big staffs, so offer to provide interview questions or even an article they can freely rewrite. Be sure to tie your article in to the needs of their readers—why would they care?

If your book is location centric—say your fictional story takes place in a small Georgia town—consider that local paper and how a story on the background to your novel will be of interest to the paper's readers and the editorial staff.

Current Event Expert

Ever wondered how those authors get on Fox News or CNN when a tragedy occurs? They may interview them about "talking to your children" about XYZ? Well, it takes planning, but you, too, can be an expert they can call. The first thing you want to do is brainstorm all of the topics you can speak to that come from your book. This isn't coming up with ways to talk about your book. It is asking yourself, "What will people learn after reading my book?" and then tying that to current events.

For instance, my book *Direction: Discernment for the Decisions of Your Life* was about spiritual discernment and knowing and doing God's will—not a topic I'd be interviewed for on Fox News. However, I looked at each chapter and distilled the lessons shared that would lend themselves to current events and created the list you can see in the Appendix.

The next step is to prepare a pitch sheet for each of those topics, because when an event happens all you have time for is to hit send. The pitch sheet needs to be created and polished ahead of time. See the Appendix for a sample.

The last step takes some research. You need a list of fax numbers—yes, this is where fax machines are still in use—for the television and radio stations that may need your expertise. Set up a Google Alert for key phrases that will notify you when an event happens so you can send that pitch sheet right away. You never know—you might be the next expert they interview.

Here are the steps for setting up a Google Alert:

1. Point your browser at Google.com/alerts.

2. Make sure you're logged into a Google account.

3. In the big blue box at the top of the page, enter the word or phrase you're looking for.

4. Click Create Alert or Show Options.

Chapter 6

Business Basics

If you went to the office of a heart surgeon and he was set up on the street corner with a folding table, handwritten signs, and his mother was manning the table, you wouldn't think much of his credentials. The same holds true for authors. If you want to be taken seriously, there are a lot of little—but important—things you must do to successfully market yourself and your book. I call these things "business basics." This chapter will discuss those basics.

Business Card

If you've been to a writers' conference, you know that a business card with your photo on it is a must. Most authors use Vistaprint, but there are many other inexpensive online card suppliers. Choose colors that match your brand, and keep the information on your card simple: your name, email address, phone number, and tagline, or just your name and Author or Author and Speaker. Ladies, don't include your home address, as that can be a safety issue.

Headshot

Get a professional headshot. Cropping other people out of a group photo you are in will not work. A picture of you from a family vacation will not work. A selfie will not work. If you want to be seen as a professional author, you need a professional headshot. Take advantage of the opportunity at writers' conferences. Ask fellow authors in your area for recommendations. Use it on your business card, for articles and online content you submit, for your website, and for that all-important back cover of the book.

Bios

Take some time to craft a series of well-written bios. Start a Word document for all of these: a version that has whimsy, one that shares a personal side, one for status, one with credentials, and one that lists everything. This last one is the one you need to update all the time; it is the one you cut and paste from to update all of the others. Your bios will vary in length and should be written in third person, not first person.

Hashtags

Develop a list of hashtags, the # sign followed by keywords, to include in your social media posts. Start a document for these and update it frequently. Hashtagify is a great tool for finding related words/tags. See the Appendix for more details on how to use a hashtag campaign.

Press Release

While a lot of marketing tips today are about using technology and having a good online presence, some things are still old school. The press release is one of those tools that works the old-fashioned way. Writing a good press release is something all writers should learn. Here's how.

1. Begin with an attention-getting headline. Just like writing the perfect book title, setting up your press release for success starts with a headline that grabs the reader's interest (in this case, the reader is who will be receiving your press release—reporters, producers, bloggers). You only have one line to work with, and most importantly, it needs to be interesting. It should not be, "Author Releases New Book." That is not newsworthy. Think about how many books are published each year. Invest the time to figure out what your hook is and use that to write a headline that is compelling.

2. Just the facts, ma'am. The first paragraph of your
    release should cover the who, what, why, where,
    and how of your hook. Reporters are inundated
    with press releases every day. They don't have a ton
    of time to sift through details and fluffy background
    information—they just need the facts that will help
    them tell your story to someone else from a position
    of authority.

3. The next paragraph is where you can give some
    background information. Tell about the author, or
    how the hook came to be. Share what you want that
    news reporter to know about why this book should
    be newsworthy.

4. Add a quote. This will draw attention, so make it
    count. The reporter may read this first and if it
    catches his/her attention they'll read the first
    paragraph next. Perhaps it's a quote from your book
    or maybe it's an endorsement from a big name.
    Don't quote a reader, because we all know someone
    who can say flowery things about our writing, so
    this is not impactful. Don't be afraid to think
    controversy: sometimes a controversial quote from

you or your book is what will make the journalist keep reading.

5. Now give the details about your book. Where it is sold, where the book signing is taking place, how to contact the author to set up an interview. End with the ISBN, and don't forget a jpeg of the book cover. If you're offering an interview, include a jpeg of yourself but make sure it is professional.

All of this must fit on a single page with enough white space that it doesn't look overwhelming. So write pithy and edit, edit, edit.

Writing a press release is only half the battle. Once you're finished creating and editing, it's time to send it out. Start local. Send it to your local newspapers, radio stations, and television stations. Make copies and hang it on bulletin boards at bookstores, coffee shops, the library, and your employee lounge. You never know who will see it. As the saying goes, we are all only six connections away from someone big.

Media Kit

Your media kit, also known as your press kit, takes some time to put together but is an important tool for building a professional outreach. Your media kit can be a physical folder, but more often than not, it will be sent digitally and is thus called an electronic press kit or EPK. An effective EPK, like its printed predecessor, is designed to help members of the media develop stories related to your business, products, or services. An EPK should contain all of the content a reporter, producer, or blogger might need to tell your story within their coverage area. Here is a list of its contents:

1. Cover letter—this will change based upon who you are sending the kit to and why. You may want to develop several: one for the media, one for speaking opportunities, one for interviews on radio or TV, and one for events.

2. Author bio and professional headshot

3. Press release

4. Endorsements

5. Author Q&A

6. Book information—back cover copy plus ordering info (ISBN, stats, reviews)

7. Excerpt from the book

Everything in your media kit should be formatted on professional letterhead that is consistent with your branding.

If you want to be taken seriously by the media, you need to provide materials that reflect a professional image. Be sure every item has your full contact information on it. There is nothing worse than gaining someone's attention and then losing out on the opportunity because they can't find how to contact you.

Business Plan

If you are going to become a professional at this writing job you need to develop a business plan. Everything worth doing is worth doing well and it is also worth investing in. Take every item in this book and decide what you will put into your plan. Next to each item determine your goal for when you wish to begin and finish each task. Finally, assign a dollar value to each item.

I wish I'd done this early on, but fortunately I wasn't too far down the road before I heard this tip. When I determined that attending writers' conferences and getting some training was what I had to do, I laid out a plan of article writing to fund my new career. I wrote a lot of twenty-dollar articles so I could pay for the conferences I attended. You can also make your wish list known to family and friends as a source of ideas of what to give you for your birthday and Christmas. God will provide if we've counted the cost and we're willing to sacrifice—just don't sacrifice your family's needs. Put first things first, and God will honor your efforts.

Ministry in Action–Cheri Cowell

We are most excited when we work with an author who has a vision of their ministry calling. One author we worked with had experience in banking and wrote a book to help Christian schools navigate the banking and loan process. He now travels the Christian schools conference circuit speaking and selling books—a lot of books. He is fulfilling his dream to further the Kingdom with his unique gifts.

Another author wrote a book sharing the stories of those who've been active in the pro-life movement. Her book funds the ministries of the people whose stories she tells—those who are serving on the front lines. Business cards are a big part of her success because they are easy to hand out on the sidewalks in front of abortion clinics.

Still another author has written a book for those struggling with addiction. She boldly put her business plan together and shared it with others who are now joining her in this important ministry. Sometimes, just putting your vision into writing is all that is needed for others to catch the vision and join hands with you.

These "business steps" may seem like busy work and not directly tied to marketing, but God can use anything, and we never know what piece of the puzzle He will use. Again, we do the work and leave the results up to God.

Chapter 7

Indie, Self, Co – Oh My!

An important decision authors have to make is choosing between traditional publishing and self-publishing. There are good reasons for both options, so you need to evaluate each one with your specific project in mind. For instance, I recently published with Zondervan, and people often ask why I would traditionally publish since I own a publishing house. Let me tell you how that came about because the story paints the picture.

I was at a writers' conference having a meal with an editor friend of mine. As we talked, she asked what I was writing on my blog lately. I told her I was doing a series on peace because it's my belief that people are looking for peace in all the wrong places and I want them to know that peace is a person. She found that interesting because her company happened to be doing a series of three books: one was on joy, one was on hope, and the third one was on peace. They were looking for someone to write that peace book that they planned to place in Cracker Barrel gift shops and restaurants. She asked if I would be interested. I smiled and said, "Yes, I think I might be."

It's important to understand that when you sign a contract with a traditional publishing house you are essentially signing away your right to use that material for the length of time that book is in publication. Those rights revert back to you when the book goes out of print. So, I wrote 365 devotions on peace that I have no access to now. I can't use them in any way—in my own marketing or writing—unless I get permission from the publisher. They're only going to give me permission to use those devotions if I am promoting that particular book.

I was willing to sign away those rights, get paid very little money, and do all of the marketing because that book is going to reach people that I have no other way to reach. People walk into Cracker Barrel and buy books off of the shelf that they wouldn't buy at a Christian bookstore. They might not find it on Amazon, but they will find it at Cracker Barrel. It is a unique ministry opportunity I was willing to make pittance on because I can reach people that I couldn't reach otherwise.

Types of Publishing

There are a lot of interchangeable terms for self-publishing, independent publishing, co-publishing, partnership publishing, and traditional publishing, and it can be confusing.

Here is how I define these terms. Self-publishing is when you do all of the work on your own. You might hire professionals to help you, such as a cover designer, an editor, and a book formatter, but you are hiring those people independently. That is true self-publishing (even though you're not doing the work entirely by yourself). There are a lot of companies that call themselves self-publishers, but they are actually independent publishers or co-publishers. The difference is that these companies provide the cover designers, illustrators, editors, and all of the people it takes to publish your book.

My company is a partnership-publishing house. I have formatters, cover designers, editors, illustrators, and marketing coaches who do all of the work for you as if you self-published or independently published. What makes us different is that we return all of the publishing rights back to you so that you own the work, and you keep 100 percent of your profits. We're in partnership with you to get your book out into the world, and to enable you to keep the money you earn in sales.

The difference between independent publishers and traditional publishers is that traditional publishers offer authors an advance against their royalties. The advance is a calculated decision based on what the publishing house believes your marketing efforts are going to produce the first year of publication. When you're putting together your book proposal, that proposal is helping the publisher determine what your advance will be if you should get a contract. It helps them determine if you are a good return on investment.

I received a $1,500 advance on my first book. That amount was based on the idea that they believed I would sell five thousand books. After my first print run, I would not make any more money until I earned out my advance. Here's where it becomes a little complicated. You would think that every book sold would count against your advance. Not exactly. My first year, I personally sold 2,500 copies of my own book. However, none of those sales counted toward my advance. The publisher made their money on my 2,500 sales, but I still needed to sell the full five thousand books via bookstore sales in order to earn back the advance.

My book retailed for $14.99, but only $0.75 of that $14.99 went toward my advance. This is the reason most authors never earn out their advance. Whatever it is that you receive as an advance is most likely all the money you will receive as a first-time author. This is also why a lot of authors are considering self-publishing, independent publishing, or partnership publishing.

Going Hybrid

In 2005, an earthquake happened in the publishing world when Amazon acquired Book Surge and Custom Flicks. Custom Flicks' name was changed to CreateSpace in 2007. In October of 2009, due to the harmonies that were created in these businesses, the CreateSpace and Book Surge brands merged under the CreateSpace name. In 2018 Kindle Direct Publishing (KDP) absorbed CreateSpace to become the publishing arm of Amazon.

This has leveled the playing field between independent authors like you and me, and the big traditional publishing houses. No longer are the publishing houses the gatekeepers to what can be published and marketed. I liken it to the change that occurred in the record business when iTunes did the same thing for recording artists that CreateSpace/KDP has done for authors.

For a while, just about anybody could publish anything and there were a lot of books published with sub-par quality—books that weren't edited well, weren't proofread, and had poorly designed covers. Self-publishing had a really bad name in the beginning.

Companies known as vanity presses began popping up to take advantage of this change in the industry. Vanity presses charged a lot of money and produced a poor product. The pendulum in self-publishing began to shift as a few high-quality self-publishing companies came on the market and operated with integrity.

About this time, an author named Paul Young had written a book called *The Shack*. He submitted the manuscript to ninety-nine publishers and was rejected by every single one. Young finally decided to take advantage of self-publishing. There are a lot of theological questions about that book, but the point of this story is that God chose to bless those self-publishing efforts.

Shortly thereafter, several other authors in the Christian publishing world—Angela Hunt, who is traditionally published with Thomas Nelson, Dan Walsh, who is traditionally published with Revell, and many others—began to explore the self-publishing world. They ushered in what is known today as the hybrid author—an author who publishes with traditional publishers and supplements their income with some self-published work. I am a hybrid author. I make the money I need with my self-published, co-published, or partnership-published books, and I traditionally publish.

Traditional vs. Independent

Now let's discuss advantages and disadvantages for independent versus traditional publishing.

With traditional publishing, the publishing house is taking all the risk. Did you know that traditional publishers are going to invest about $45,000 to publish a first-time author? That is, they are going to invest $45,000 not just to publish your book, but also to market your book and launch your career as an author. That is a huge investment.

If you are independently publishing (I'm using the terms self-publishing and independent publishing interchangeably here), you are going to personally invest the money and take the risk. The good news is you don't need to spend $45,000 to do that. Your budget can range anywhere from $1,000 to $10,000 with independent publishing.

For some people, taking on the risk is freeing and exhilarating; for others, taking that risk is scary. That in itself might tell you which publishing option is right for you.

With a traditional publishing contract, you will be assigned a designer who will make the decisions regarding your book cover. You might have some input as a first-time author, but you will not have the final say. You won't even have the final say on your book title. The final title for my book *Direction, Discernment for the Decisions of Your Life* was nothing like the title I had originally chosen. I was happy with the new title; however, I did not like the cover design they created.

With self-publishing, you make all of the decisions. This can be good and bad. Even though my company has hundreds of books under its belt and lots of experience and expertise, if authors are married to their cover concept, they're going to stick with it. Sometimes they're right, but some-times they're not.

Now let's talk about profits. With a traditional book contract, I've already shared the concept of the advance. The advance is often all you will ever make, but if you are blessed enough to earn out your advance you are going to make about a 12 percent royalty on your books, which

MARKETING AS MINISTRY

averages out to be about one to two dollars profit on the sale of every book. With independent publishing, you are making 100 percent of the profit. With some partnership-publishing houses you will make between four and seven dollars in profit. If you publish with us, you will make ten to fifteen dollars in profit off the sale of every book. When Amazon or one of the other business partners sells the book on your behalf, you will earn 40 percent, not the 12 percent that I make with my traditionally published books. It is a major difference on the profit side. If you want to make a higher profit, then independent publishing is the way to go.

Let's talk about the big elephant in the room—the negative reputation associated with self-publishing. Traditional publishing is going to get you prestige. When you can say you've been contracted with Zondervan or Thomas Nelson, that carries some clout. The good news is that there isn't as much stigma attached to independent publishing today as there was a decade ago. If you choose a partnership publisher like EABooks, your book will not say CreateSpace or KDP on it. It will say, "Published by EABooks Publishing," so it won't look self-published in any way. If you are trying to get a contract with an independent

113

publishing house, be sure to ask what name will appear on your book.

When you are traditionally published, the editing is handled in-house. An editor will review your book and you will receive what's known as a galley proof with the editor's suggested revisions. That galley proof is your one chance to make the editorial revisions. You might be able to push back a little on the editor's suggestions, but more likely than not you will need to accept the changes.

At larger publishing houses, there will be several more editing opportunities to review your book, but at a smaller house you have just one. With independent publishing, there is no limit. There is a misconception that the reason why there are errors in books today is because they are self-published. That is not the case. Every single one of my traditionally published books has errors in it. There is no way to eliminate every error. So, for all of the melancholy authors out there who are striving for perfection, I want you to get rid of that desire from your mind because you are never, ever, ever going to publish a perfect manuscript. There will always be errors. The good news is that when you publish with us we can easily fix those errors, re-upload your manuscript, and get a new, more perfected version out there. If you are traditionally publishing, you need to get through your full print run first before you can fix any errors.

Chapter 8

Questions to Ask Yourself

In the previous chapter we discussed the different types of publishing and some of the pros and cons of each. There are a lot of options out there and it can feel overwhelming, especially for first-time authors. There are some questions you need to ask yourself that will help you determine which publishing path is best for you. Let's discuss those now.

What Is Your Why?

When you are deciding whether to traditionally publish or go the partnership-publishing or self-publishing route, the first question to ask yourself is why you are publishing your book. Many people roll their eyes at me when I ask that question, but it is essential.

I had published my third traditionally published book and my wonderful husband had taken me out to dinner to celebrate. Sitting across the table from me, he asked, "Cheri, when are you finally going to admit that you are a successful author?" I looked back at him and thought, That is a *great question.* I had been chasing the dream of being a successful author, but I had never determined what that would look like.

If you are chasing an undetermined target you are never going to reach that target. What measurement of success are you going to use? Do you want to see your name on a book, in a bookstore, on the shelf? If that is your measurement of success, then self-publishing or partnership-publishing is not going to get you to that goal.

Is your measurement of success to make a certain dollar amount, or receive an email from someone that says they just finished reading your book and it changed their life? Is it simply to be obedient to the calling that God has given you? In other words, do you know God has called you to share your message and you will do whatever it takes to get that message out there as a demonstration in obedience? If any of these are your measurement of success, then you could achieve that through self-publishing or partnership-publishing. You need to be honest with yourself and set the goal. If you never set the goal, you will never achieve it.

Who Is This For?

Another question to ask yourself is, who is your target market. I thought that my target market was forty-five to sixty-five-year-olds who attend church, who might not have a solid biblical foundation, who want to study the Bible so they can grow in their faith and their relationship with Jesus, but who might be missing some of the key understandings of Bible stories and Bible lessons. I did not think my target market was reading e-books.

I thought I understood my target market until my husband and I went on an Alaskan cruise. We were celebrating our twenty-fifth wedding anniversary and we were the youngest people on the ship. It seemed everybody else had already celebrated their fiftieth wedding anniversary and they thought my husband and I were cute. One evening we were walking on the deck and I was shocked to see so many of these older people reading from their Kindles. I realized I had my target audience wrong.

I went home after that cruise and sent out a survey asking my readers if they buy books at a Christian bookstore or from Amazon, and if they buy print books or e-books. I was amazed at what I learned. Eighty-five percent of people buy books from Amazon. That means only 15 percent of people are buying books in a traditional bookstore. And my readers were no different.

The question then becomes, where is your target market shopping. That is key to knowing which publishing direction is most advantageous for you and your book. Is a traditional publisher, whose major market is the bookstore, the right way for you to go? Or is your target market shopping on Amazon like 85 percent of the people out there?

A fourth question to ask yourself is if you have a way for people to see your book. If your target market is that bookstore reader, how are you going to convince people to make a trip to the bookstore to buy your book off of the shelf? It is a common misunderstanding of traditional publishing to think that the publisher will get people into the bookstore to buy your book. They will not. They are going to get a few people in there, but the majority of your book sales, even through a traditional publisher, are going to be based on your marketing efforts. How are you going to get people into that bookstore to buy your book? On the flip side of that is, how are you going to convince your reader to go to Amazon or your website and buy your book. I am assuming that is why you are reading this book, so refer back to Chapter 2 for the answer to this question.

Who Has Your Rights?

The last question to consider is whether or not you have the e-book rights for your out-of-print book. This is relevant for authors who have traditionally published, or those who have self-published and want to know if there is a way to republish. To answer this question, review your contract to see who has the rights to your book and understand what you can do to get your rights back if your traditional publishing house still holds those rights.

I will be honest with you. I cannot get the e-book rights for the first book I published even though I own a partnership-publishing house that specializes in e-books. The reason is because my book is still in print, and when I signed the contract, I signed away all of my rights. As long as that book is in print, I cannot get my rights back to publish that book in e-book format.

Should You DIY?

If you've decided you want to go the self-publishing, independent publishing, or partnership-publishing route, the big question is, should you hire someone like us, or should you do it yourself? There is no need to pay money for what you can do yourself, but there are some questions that will help you decide which option is best for you. The first one is, how computer literate are you?

Most authors use Microsoft Word to type their manuscripts and have learned how to do standard manuscript formatting. In other words, you know to use twelve-point font, you can select Times New Roman, and you can even number your pages. But if the tab key were eliminated from your keyboard, would you know how to type your manuscript including headers and subheads? E-books need to be created without code, which Microsoft Word tends to add automatically behind the scenes. Do you know how to check for that? If the answers to these questions are no, then you probably need to hire someone.

Do you know how to set your spacing before and after a paragraph? Do you know how to set your indentation lines? Do you know how set a hanging paragraph without using the tab key? If you don't know how to accomplish these things without using the tab key, you need to hire someone.

Something else to ask yourself is how much time you have to learn the ropes. If you are only publishing one book, then you have time to learn how to self-publish. But if you believe God has called you to write multiple books, you might want to spend your available time writing and not learning all of the steps in the publishing process.

Likewise, as we discussed in Chapter 4, you should consider how much your time is worth. You could learn the things already mentioned, but that might not be the best use of your time. Perhaps it is more worthwhile to pay someone to produce the book so you can focus on writing, marketing, ministering to readers, and connecting with them on a deep level.

DIY Options

If you choose to do it yourself, you have several options. Amazon's self-publishing platform, CreateSpace, recently merged with KDP (Kindle Direct Publishing) and is focused on print books. Another option for print is Lightning Source, an independent publishing platform that was started by a distributor for traditional publishing houses. They work differently than CreateSpace/KDP and they're not as user-friendly. They have a different royalty program and they are focused on getting your books into bookstores. IngramSpark is another option similar to Lightning Source. Ingram was a distributor for traditional publishing houses to the bookstore market; IngramSpark is their self-publishing platform, but it has a steep learning curve to properly format your book. These are the three most common options for self-publishing.

There are some challenges with each option, and it depends on how computer savvy you are as to whether or not you can overcome those challenges. If you are an average author who uses Microsoft Word to type your manuscript, I strongly encourage you to find a professional to format your book. If you want to load your files directly to KDP you can do that. There may be a formatting fee involved, so be sure to look into that.

For authors who are publishing an e-book, Smashwords is a popular option. Mark Corker, the genius who enabled independent publishers to compete in the e-book market with traditional publishing houses, started Smashwords. Smashwords gives you access to Kobo, the international market for e-books, or you can publish directly through Kobo. Kindle is Amazon's e-book platform. The newest e-book publishing option is Walmart. Smashwords is working with Walmart to offer e-books in competition with Amazon. Again, there are pros and cons for each of these e-book options. You can research them fully on their individual websites. It took me four months of working with my techie friend to get my first e-book published—it was a lot more difficult than I'd been led to believe.

There are a lot of publishers on the broad spectrum—from independent, partnership, and co-publishing. There are only a few I feel comfortable recommending to authors. Unfortunately, just hanging a shingle out that says, "Christian publisher," does not mean they operate from an ethical, integrity-filled standpoint. That is sad to say. The best advice I can give is to find out what Christian writers' conferences they attend, because Christian writers' conferences have become the gatekeepers for these publishers. Also, keep in mind that just because someone is affiliated with a big Christian publisher does not mean they are ethical.

If the publishers are not represented at Christian writers' conferences on a regular basis, if they are not being invited back year after year, that might be a good sign you need to look elsewhere.

Questions to Ask before You Sign a Contract

Before you sign a contract with a publisher, ask what their royalties are and if they are paid off of net or gross sales. This will give you a clear insight as to how much money you will actually make. With our publishing house you get 100 percent of the profits when you sell the book yourself, and 40 percent if you sell through Amazon or one of the other distributors we work with.

You need to find out if your contract is exclusive or non-exclusive—if you will be prevented from signing agreements with anyone else. For instance, Paul Young had the rights to *The Shack* so he could shop his book anywhere. That's why publishers were coming to him after he sold so many books on his own.

You also need to ask about your ISBN. Who it is registered to will determine the name of the publisher that will appear on your book. Make sure the ISBN number is registered with a publishing house and that it will be in your name.

You also need to ask if the publishing house were to go out of business, will you own your files, and are they production-ready. In 2018 there was a high-profile publisher named Tate Publishing that went out of business. The owner was imprisoned for fraud and embezzlement. Unfortunately, almost all of the authors did not have production-ready files. This publishing house—that called itself a Christian publishing company—embedded a signature in the files so authors could not use them to reproduce their books. Authors had to recreate the files if they wanted to republish their books. You need to make sure you are receiving production-ready files—not PDF files—including your cover. You also want all file copies—the InDesign files and any jpeg files for your cover.

Ask to talk to an author who has been published by the publishing house you're considering signing a contract with. Ask to see samples of the covers the publisher has designed and books they have published. Ask where your books will sell, who the main distributors are, and who is on the expanded distribution list. Find out to whom your book will be available.

You want to know how many author copies will be included or need to be purchased when you sign the contract. We do not have a requirement like that, but many publishing houses do. It does not mean it is a bad contract, but you want to understand how many copies you are obligated to buy.

Find out how much your book will cost when you go to order your book to resell it. This is called the author cost. For us, your book is going to cost anywhere between two and four dollars when you buy the book to resell it. With my traditionally published books, I cannot get my books for less than $7.50. You need to know how much your book will cost you because that will make a difference in how much your profit is. Also ask who sets your retail price. Some of my competitors set their authors' retail price, limiting the amount of profit that authors can make. We do not do this.

Ask for a list of all of the add-ons and extras the publishing house might require of you. What I see happen often is after an author has signed a contract, the publisher comes back with upcharges they "forgot" to mention that were not included in the contract. The author ends up doubling the amount they expected to spend because they were not informed of extras that would be required once they published.

Ask about your order fulfillment options. When you order a book, how is that order going to be fulfilled? If you are speaking at an event, can you have those books drop-shipped to the venue? Or will they be shipped to your home or office address and you are responsible for either shipping them to the venue or carrying them in an additional suitcase, which you will have to pay extra for? You need to understand how the fulfillment will work.

Will there be one person assigned to answer your questions? This is huge, because as you go through the self-publishing process, there are a gazillion decisions that need to be made. If you are not assigned one person as your project coordinator to answer those questions and help walk you through the process, you could be left hanging. We have worked with authors who have come to us after publishing their first book with a company that did not match them with a dedicated project coordinator. When they would call the publisher to ask questions, they spoke with a different person—who often was not familiar with their book—each time. Find out if you will have one person assigned to you and how you will be able to reach them. Are they only available via email? Are they only available on Mondays between 2:00 p.m. and 4:00 p.m. Pacific time? If you are someone who prefers to have a dedicated contact person to answer questions and walk you through the process, you may want to consider a partnership-publishing house.

How long is the publication process of the company you're considering? And what can extend that process? Our publication process is 120 days from the time we receive your manuscript to the time it is fully published. For us, the author is what extends the process. Some authors take longer than others to review their galley proof and make corrections. Also, some authors are more available than others for answering questions and other behind-the-scenes work. Those are examples of what can slow things down for us, but you need to find out from the publishing house you're considering working with what their publication process is and what things tend to slow that down.

How will your marketing support work? What exactly is this publisher going to do for you? How much will it cost? I hear from a lot of authors that other publishers make lofty promises with regard to marketing their book. Publishers claim they have a sales team that will visit all of the bookstores. What that really means is they have a catalog and your book will be included in that catalog. If it's an independent publishing house, once that salesperson drops off the catalog—that beautiful marketing piece you have paid for—it is going in the circular file, which is another word for trashcan. Beware of the slick, fancy marketing support some publishers will try to sell you. The reality is, your book is not going to be in a Christian bookstore sitting on a shelf if you are self- or independently published. It's just not going to happen.

We help our authors get their books into Christian bookstores with shoe leather. We show them how to work with local Christian bookstores, but it is really the author's efforts that will get their book on the shelf. There is not a self-publisher out there that can promise you your book will be in a Christian bookstore, so beware of those that do.

Finally, you need to know how a contract termination is handled. There needs to be something in your contract that protects you and something that protects the publisher should either one of you decide at any point that the relationship is not working. There needs to be a termination clause and you need to understand exactly how it will be handled.

At EABooks Publishing, we are expanding our publishing options to include packages for every budget and that include all of the considerations such as distribution and bookstore availability that we've outlined in this chapter. The lower-cost packages have fewer bells and whistles, while the most expensive ones have everything you could want. Remember that what your mother told you is true: you get what you pay for, and if it sounds too good to be true, it probably is. So, check us out and if you see one of my independent publishing friends at a conference, check out what they offer. Then pray about it and know you are in good hands. Each of us is here for you.

Change Your Mindset

We've talked about why it's important to change your mindset from author to reader as you put together the marketing plan for your book. Now, I want to discuss changing your mindset from being the author to being the publisher. Whether you hire us or someone else, you are putting on the hat of publisher. What that means is you will need to pay attention to every detail that is required to publish your book from start to finish. We walk our authors through every one of those steps and help them make informed decisions. If, however, you choose to publish on your own, it is imperative that you begin to think like a publisher. For instance, let's talk about your cover.

When thinking like an author, you are concerned with the message you have to share in your book. You want that message conveyed on your cover. When you put your publisher hat on, you need to think about how to design the cover so it will interest the reader enough that they want to flip the book over and read the back-cover copy. The cover is not just a place to promote your message. It is an aspect of marketing your book and it needs to be intriguing so the reader wants to look at the back cover and learn more. Then, as the publisher, you want to think about how that back-cover copy will resonate with the reader enough to make them want to open the book and read the table of contents.

As the publisher, you want to make sure that the table of contents doesn't just list the chapter titles, but that those chapter titles hook the reader enough that they begin reading the introduction or the first paragraphs of the first chapter, because that is where the decision is made to buy the book.

Your book cover is just one of many aspects in the publishing process where you will need to change your mindset from author to publisher. Thinking like the publisher means looking at your book in a way that will engage the reader on a deeper level and cause them to want to buy the book.

Common Causes of Failure

One of the common causes of failure authors make with publishing their book is the "if you build it, they will come" mentality. They think if they just publish a book it will be a success — people are going to find it, fall in love with it, buy it, and tell all of their friends to buy it. That mentality is not true. If you publish a book, it is one of thousands upon thousands of books that are also competing for readers' attention. Having a book, a website, and a Facebook account doesn't guarantee people will find your book.

How do you overcome that common cause of failure? By connecting to your readers' hopes, dreams, fears, and faith questions. When you connect to someone on that deeper level, you are connecting on a heart level that is longer lasting than anything else. When you do this, they will begin to tell their family and friends about your website, about how your book is speaking to them, and about how you as the author are speaking their language, meeting their needs, and answering their questions. That's how to combat the "if you build it, they will come" mentality.

Another common cause of failure is thinking like an author and not a reader. This is a big shift many authors who self-publish or partnership publish need to make. You must take off your author hat, which is what you've been wearing to write your book and put on a reader hat or a publisher hat. That means you are constantly thinking from the readers' perspective. What are my readers' questions? What are my readers' needs? Where are my readers shopping? What magazines are my readers reading? How am I going to connect to my readers so that they want to buy the book?

This is the magic behind the way we approach our author websites. Our marketing coaches create an environment where readers can connect with the author on a meaningful level and want to buy the author's book. Not because the author is selling it or promoting it, but because the author has ministered to readers and met their needs.

Another common cause of failure is putting all your eggs in one marketing basket. When I meet with an author, they want to know what the secret is to marketing success. That secret doesn't exist. What I tell them is not to put everything in one basket. The mistake is thinking that having a website, or a Facebook page, or landing that one radio interview will be the key to their success. It is not one single thing that is going to do it for you. What has worked for me is doing a broad spectrum of basic things and then doing the next thing on my list with excellence. That is the secret.

We only have twenty-four hours a day. We have family and church responsibilities; we are involved in activities for our own health and spiritual well-being. We add to that marketing, writing, and being faithful to the calling that God has place on us. Yet, we can't do everything at once. Going back to the concept of the cake and icing or laying the foundation for the house, we need to get the basics done first. Then when it comes to marketing, we need to resist putting all of our eggs in one basket. Don't think there is one silver bullet and if you can just do that one thing it will make all the difference, because there isn't one miracle thing.

The last common cause of failure we'll discuss is the biggest one — discouragement. Satan knows he can discourage us if he can get us focused on our Amazon ranking, our book sales, our bank account, our to-do list that never seems to go away, our mistakes, our failures at measuring up to whatever ideal we think we should be reaching or comparing ourselves to. I certainly have authors I could easily measure myself against and I would fail every time. If you're comparing yourself to someone else, Satan is going to use that to discourage you. Discouragement is the tool he uses to stop you from fulfilling your calling.

What is the best way to combat discouragement? Have a circle of author friends who understand you. The best place to do that is at writers' conferences. Meeting fellow authors who are on the journey with you might be the best thing you do at a writers' conference. Your family is not going to completely understand this crazy world that we live in, but your fellow authors will. When you get discouraged, all you need to do is send a note to one of those authors and say, "I am feeling like a total failure today." That author will know what you are feeling, come alongside you, lift you up, and get your eyes refocused on all the right things.

Chapter 9

A Word of Encouragement

I have given you a lot of information and ideas in a relatively short number of pages. You can implement as few of these things or as many of them as you want. My goal was to show you that you don't have to feel guilty when it comes to marketing your book, because marketing truly is a ministry. I also wanted to help you see how you can make this manageable in your own life, because, honestly, I really did beat myself up for not posting on social media each day that first week after my conference. I really did need to figure out a way to make this work for me, and my cell phone is not connected to my hip bone. It is not the first thing I think about. When I see something fabulous, I don't think about posting it on my Facebook page. I think about calling my mom and telling her about it. I think about praising God; I just stop in the middle of the road and say, "God, that is an amazing moon."

This book is for authors like me who want to do the things we're told we need to do in order to attract readers.

We all have family and friends who will buy our books, but after we have exhausted those resources, we have to reach out further. We have to find other people out there. After all, isn't that what we're about as Christians? We're about going out into the world. I am amazed how far my message has gone with Facebook. I don't know the majority of the people who follow me, but they believe they know me. I am amazed because I've connected with some of them in a way that when they're in crisis they reach out to me and I've prayed over those situations.

Why are they reaching out to me? Because I've met their needs in other ways, and I'm safe. They can tell me that their teenage son just declared that he is a homosexual. They ask, "What do I do? How do I handle this?" They're not yet ready to tell their pastor. They don't want to tell their best friend. They don't know what to say. They think I have answers because I've written on homosexuality. I know the answer because I know the One who has all the answers. You also know the One who has all the answers.

Start Small

I heard from an author who didn't have a website or a blog. She had a personal Facebook page and that was about it. She had a full-time job that required her to travel, so she didn't have twenty hours a week to devote to marketing her book. Her question was, "Where should I start?"

If you find yourself in a similar situation, or if you're suffering from analysis paralysis because of all the possibilities on how to market your book, I suggest you start with either your Facebook page or your website. The key to building your audience is consistency. If you say you're going to post on Facebook or your blog every other week, you need to post every other week. Your readers will get used to your schedule and expect that, so you want to be consistent. Take it easy on yourself and don't beat yourself up for not doing everything I'm suggesting in this book all at once. What I'm sharing with you is like the Cadillac version. Maybe you're at a Yugo level or a bicycle level. That is okay.

Start where you are, but at the least, now that you've read this book, you know where you're going. I've been doing this since the year 2000. You can't get to where I am from day one. It took me a long time to figure all of this out. I spent a lot of money and did a lot of things wrong. I'm showing you the easy way because I don't want you to make the same mistakes I did. Start out small and be good at one thing first. Then slowly add the next thing once you have the first thing mastered, and then slowly add the next thing.

If you need help, then reach out. We are here for you at EABooks Publishing, and there are many others in our industry who want to help you reach your goals. Some of you are quite capable of reading this book and taking the bull by the horns — accomplishing all of this step-by-step. However, many of you are realizing this is beyond your comfort zone. You feel you could do all of this but the thought of doing it yourself makes you break out in a cold sweat. This is a sure sign you need to hire a coach. Just be sure that at the end of the contract you will be able to continue on your own. In other words, the process should help you to stand on your own two feet, fully trained in what to do next and how to do it without having to pay more money.

Overwhelmed?

I want to encourage those of you who are feeling overwhelmed. That is a common feeling among authors. We live in an exciting time where advances in technology are giving us more and more opportunities to connect with our readers, communicate our message, and market our book. It's happening at a fast pace, and it's giving us a lot of choices. This can be good and bad. It is wonderful to have options, but it's also easy to get overwhelmed the point where we get stuck and we don't make any decisions at all.

After feeling like I would never master this part of writing, I wrote an article titled "From A Weary Marketer." If you are one of those weary marketers and you've read through this whole book and you are just feeling overwhelmed, I want to leave you with this bit of advice. Don't feel that you have to do all of this all at once in order to be successful. This is a lifelong journey, and I invite you to go at the pace that is good for you. Just do the next thing on the list and do it with excellence.

Join Hands

Finally, may I encourage you to find a few friends for the journey, because all Christian authors are in this together. We are all pulling on the same team. We all work for the same Team Captain. At the end of the road, all of us want to hear the words, "Well done, good and faithful servant."

It is a good journey. It is joy-filled journey. It is a journey worth the effort, and I know it will be full of fruit, not only for you, but also for the Kingdom.

Appendix

The Marketing Pyramid

By
Cheri Cowell

The Marketing Pyramid

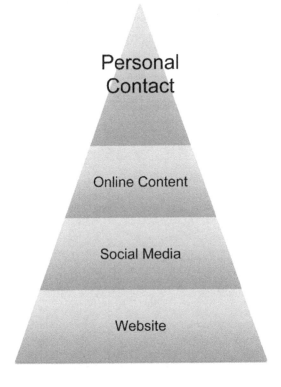

The foundation is your website—the destination for all marketing—it is where you meet readers' needs.

Social media—drives traffic to your website where ministry happens

Online content—blogs, articles, resources where you contribute and where you connect your readers to great content for their benefit

Personal contact—where you meet readers in person such at signings, readings, fairs, speaking events, God-incidences, workshops, teas, and fundraisers

Using #Hashtag Marketing to Drive Sales

Why #Hashtag Marketing?

Simply—because engaged customers are loyal customers.

So What Are We Talking About?

Hashtags are a word or group of words after the # sign (like "#hashtag"). After used in a post on Twitter, Instagram, Pinterest, and Facebook, clicking on these hashtags will show you all other messages that contain the same hashtag. A successful hashtag campaign can create a community of engaged individuals. Remember: engaged customers are loyal customers.

There are two types of campaigns:

1. Brand Hashtags are more long-term and improve the search engine optimization of your brand. They also get your updates seen by your consumers who are searching for, or using, the hashtag words. An example would be #Name of Store New Releases because it is something that happens on a regular basis.

149

2. Campaign hashtags are unique to a short-term contest or promotion. An example of these would be #Name of Store Bible Studies for Fall, # Name of Store New Year Devotion, or # Name of Store Easter is for Kids.

So, How Do You Create a Hashtag Campaign?

The first thing you want to do is research your potential hashtag word or phrase. On Twitter, enter your word or phase in the search box, then click *More Options*. Choose, *Tweets From Everyone and From Everywhere*. Read through these to be sure your hashtag has not been taken or does not have some other meaning that you don't intend.

Next, click on *Advanced Search* under *More Options* to more narrowly define your hashtag. You will want to keep your hashtag short and make it memorable.

Now that you have your hashtag, create a post to explain it and encourage others to use it.

Examples of # Name of Store New Year Devotion:
#RainbowsNewYearDevo www.RainbowsBooks.com/Devo

Most devotional books are sold to start the New Year off right with God's Word. Here is the post you might write for your Facebook page: Start the New Year off with Devotion to God's Word. Share how you use a daily devo to anchor your day. # Name of Store New Year Devotion (Link to website page where new devo books are highlighted.)

Twitter: Share how you use a daily devo to anchor your day to God's Word. # Name of Store New Year Devotion (Link to website page where new devo books are highlighted.)

Often-overlooked Opportunities to Get Published (and Get Paid)

Ask yourself:

1. **What am I already involved in?** sports, children, reading, scrapbooking

2. **Who can I serve?** List your experiences and lessons learned

3. **How am I gifted?** Leader, prayer, witnessing, talkative

4. **Why am I doing this?** Money, credits, expert, grow/expand

Reviews — Christian retailing, local paper, websites

- Books, movies, music, videos, websites, dramas, concerts

Curriculum — denominational

- Sunday school (all ages), Bible study, small group, youth, home-school

Gift/Specialty Market — poetry, muse, companion products

- Greeting cards, games, gifts, journals, software, novelty, toys

Newspapers — letter to editor, expert

- Local, specialty, regional

- Opinion, editorials, columns

Trade Magazines — home improvement, gardening, travel

- What are your interests?

Profiles/Celebrity Pieces — for your byline

Photos — for added interest

- With and without an article

Fillers and Sidebars — for your byline

- Puzzles, games, crafts, anecdotes, cartoons, facts, ideas, jokes, prayers, quizzes, quotes, sermon illustrations, humor, tips, word puzzles, recipes

Short Stories — 300 to 500 words

- Adventure, allegory, biblical, contemporary, ethnic, fantasy, frontier/romance, historical/romance, humorous, juvenile, literary, mystery/romance, parables, plays, romance, science fiction, senior adult fiction, skits, speculative, teen/young adult, Westerns

Possible Current Event Tie-ins to *Direction*

Tragedy/Suffering – From Chapter 2: Is There an Obstacle or Opposition?

The "Why, God, Why?" question

Squaring a loving God with a suffering world

Trusting a God who allows suffering

The danger of seeing God as too big or too small

Poor Choices – From Chapter 3: Is It God-sized?

More than a WWJD bracelet

The danger of seeing God as too big or too small

Developing wisdom muscles

National Day of Prayer/ See You at the Pole/9-11 – From Chapter 7: Obstacles to Hearing from God

Six key obstacles hindering our prayers

Hearing God's voice

Distinguishing God's voice from our own

False division of sacred and secular/church and state

Economy/Finances/Decision-Making – From Chapter 8: Asking the Wrong Question

Discernment for the Decisions of Your life

Goal setting God's way

Aligning our wills with His

Developing wisdom muscles in . . .

Choice overload – too many choices, too many voices

Illusion of Control/Security – From Chapter 4: Does It Require Steps of Faith?

Meet the self-sisters

Security is one of Satan's most effective lies

Patriotism-Freedom/Faith in Action – From Chapter 1: Is this Aligned with the Character of God?

Faith is an action word – three components

Collision of kingdoms

Current Event Pitch Sheet Sample

Attention (news editor):

Current Event Expert

Event: (Tragedy at Central High)

Author and Speaker: Cheri Cowell

As our community wrestles with the events that took place at Central High, many are seeking answers to what author Cheri Cowell writes and speaks on—the Why, God, Why Question. This question gets at the heart of the human need to explain why such suffering occurs, and how we can trust once again. In answering this question Cheri uncovers three faulty views often turned to in times like these:

1. View One: God doesn't want me to be happy

2. View Two: God is punishing me

3. View Three: God has willed it

The answer: living in tension between where we are now and our final state on the other side of life. It is what theologians call an "already not yet" theology.

Habakkuk, a prophet and the author of one of the last books of the Old Testament, asked questions, a lot of questions, and God answers Habakkuk's questions — and ours. God does not explain the whys and hows of suffering, but He does promise that in the end evil will be conquered. It is this hope to which we must cling now.

Cheri Cowell's Bio

Author, speaker, and theological student Cheri Cowell lives in Orlando, Florida with her husband Randy. She has written numerous articles for magazines and contributed to several collections including *Groovy Chick's Road Trip to Peace* and *Chicken Soup for the Grandma's Soul*. Her published books include *Direction: Discernment for the Decisions of Your Life*. With wisdom garnered from her years serving in the local church, and now in her studies at Asbury Theological Seminary (Orlando campus) Cheri speaks to the deep questions of life and faith with warmth and an eye toward practical applications in life.

Evergreen Article Ideas

Most publications request these *seasonal articles* to be submitted four to six, even twelve months in advance. Check the writer's guidelines and consider writing them this year and submitting for the next.

January

Pressing forward, looking back
Goal setting
Organization
Debt
Scrap booking
Epiphany
MLK
Winter/depression
Keeping kids busy on snow days
Losing weight
Exercise
Superbowl

February

Love (all kinds)
President's Day
Groundhog Day; repeats
Dealing with regrets
Ash Wednesday
Brotherhood/sisterhood week

March

Spring cleaning
World day of prayer
St. Patrick's Day
Easter
Organization
Garage sales
Summer camps research

April

April Fools' Day; truth
Taking jokes too far
Good/clean fun
Taxes
Stewardship
Money savers
Secretary's Day
Passover
April showers — bridal, baby showers
Arbor Day — creation ethics

May

National Day of Prayer
Graduations
New leaves — growth
How to take good pictures
Holocaust remembrance
Christian/Jewish relations
Mother's Day
Armed Forces Day
Memorial Day
Vacation planning
Family reunions

June

Flag Day
Patriotism
Summer fun
Service projects
Family time
Father's Day
Devotional time
VBS
Backyard Bible clubs

July

Independence
Faith of our Forefathers
Parent's Day
US history

August

Friendship Sunday
Back to school
Planning for high school
Deciding on a college
Church planning

September

9/11
Feast of Tabernacles
Labor Day
Grandparent's Day
Fall — death and dying
Sportsmanship

October

World communion Sunday
Clergy appreciation
Rosh Hashanah
Yom Kippur
All Saints Day
Halloween
Evil
Festivals

November

Election day
Politics
Veteran's Day
National Bible Sunday
Thanksgiving
Recipes
Holiday parties
Advent
Family relations
Reaching out to others
Pilgrims and our heritage

December

Pearl Harbor Day
Advent
Christmas
New Year's resolutions
Goal setting

Print Book Reviews

This is a list of review sites for print books. Many also accept independently published books. I do not endorse any of these sites, as some are general (secular) market sites. Every author must determine for themselves where they draw the line for being in the world but not of it as a Christian author.

http://www.tmycann.com Fantasy, sci fi, romance, mystery, historical fiction

http://www.abookloverslibrary.com/

http://alifeamongthepages.wordpress.com/

http://www.alustforreading.com/ Romance

http://ashleysbookshelf.blogspot.com/

http://awesomeindies.net/

http://gabixlerreviews-bookreadersheaven.blogspot.com/

http://www.tc-bookedup.blogspot.com/

http://blog.booksontheknob.org

http://breakoutbooks.blogspot.com/

http://readitreviewit.wordpress.com/

http://www.emptymirrorbooks.com/ Art and poetry

http://fantasybookcritic.blogspot.com/ Fantasy

http://www.imafulltimemummy.com/page/My-Book-
Reviews.aspx Children, parenting, family, Christian

https://indiefic.wordpress.com/ Fiction

http://indiekindleblitz.wordpress.com/

http://christianreads.blogspot.com/ Christian

http://littlehyuts.blogspot.com/ YA

http://lucybirdbooks.wordpress.com/ Contemporary
and Historical Fiction

http://www.mommasaysread.com/ Fiction

http://www.regrom.com/ Romance

http://www.rosebuz.com/ Christian Fiction

E-Book Reviews

Many of the print book sites do not review e-books. This is a list of currently available sources to have your e-book reviewed or listed for promotion. Some are free, while some charge a membership fee. I do not endorse any of these as some are general market (secular) sites and some content may be offensive. Every author must determine for their own books how much salt and light they wish to be in the world. We are told we are to be in the world but not of the world, and that is a decision between you and God.

Goodreads

Use your free membership to promote yourself and your books. Reviews are essential and reviews on Goodreads site help your book to really stand out to millions of visitors.

Wattpad

Wattpad has experienced explosive growth since its inception and has become the world's most popular destination to publish and read e-books. Wattpad delivers billions of pages from its library of works created and published by the Wattpad community.

BookTalk.org

You'll find an online reading group and book discussion forum that can help you discover new books. If you are an author or publisher looking to promote your books, you are welcome to use BookTalk.org as a tool to reach a vast audience of book lovers. They have a Google Page Rank of 5, over 14,000 members and close to 700,000 site views per month. Book discussion forums are free and open to anyone including authors and publishers. Create a free account and write about your books in either the Fiction Book Forum or Non-Fiction Book Forum. Mail a few copies of your print book and it will be advertised. They will advertise your book on the Home page for fifteen to thirty days and on the Featured Book Suggestions page permanently.

Booktalk.com

An online booklovers' community composed of many of today's bestselling and popular authors. Personalized author home pages contain excerpts from bestselling novels as well as information about upcoming releases, author notes and personal hobbies and interests as well as publisher, literary agent, and book industry information. Writing related articles by Booktalk authors and others in the writing community and upcoming literary events are also included.

Library Thing

Social networking site and forum for book lovers. Free profile where each book contains tags, reviews, and links to conversations about the book.

WritersNet

List yourself at this writers and authors directory, sorted by genre or location. Various resources for writers, agents and publishers.

Bibliophil

Forum about books. Offers: profile with books appearing in signature, list of favorite and wished books.

Booksie

Share Your poems, short stories, novels, and more with the world. Sign up, it's free.

BookBrowse

Selected book listing, authors interviews, link to authors' website; reviewed by humans, not all books accepted, check submission guidelines.

Nothing Binding

Upload and manage your book cover image and book promotion materials. Showcase your work for free: writings, books, articles, short stories, essays, poems, and more.

Book Buzzr

Has a thirty-day free trial listing and a paid listing with monthly payment of under $5.

Bookhitch

Free listing: a sixty-word description and five keywords per book. Premium listing: $19.95/year—120 words description and space for book reviews. An educational resource that connects you to the work of more than 200,000 authors, illustrators, publishers, and other creators of books for children and young adults.

Scribd

Find out what others are reading on Scribd. This service is somewhat comparable with Wattpad. Authors upload their PDF, Word, and PowerPoint docs to share them with the world's largest community of readers.

WhoWroteWhat.net

Authors can advertise free for thirty days. Submit a portrait photo (jpg), up to fifty words inviting readers to your website, and your URL where your book(s) are for sale. After thirty days it is as low as twenty-seven cents a day.

SavvyBookWriters Blog

Our marketing clients' books and author bio are posted here on this blog, plus we will have an interview with them, published here, too. Both articles will stay forever on our site, free of charge.

Bookreportradio

A lively mix of author interviews, audio book previews, and chats with those influential in the literary world, The Book Report has become appointment listening for bibliophiles and book clubs alike.

Tim Greaton Forum

Tim Greaton is presenting the most talented authors & artists, living and working in our world today.

Author Marketing Club

No longer do you have to dig up your links to the best places to submit your books. We've put them all together here for you in one spot.

Books on The Knob

Bargain reads, free e-books and book reviews for the Amazon Kindle, nook, Kobo, Sony and other e-readers, Kindle Fire, nookColor, Kobo Vox, and other tablets, along with some games, music, technology, and computers tossed in now and then.

Digital Book Today

Includes both free and paid options for writers looking to promote.

E-books Habit

Each day we will bring you twenty to thirty great e-books that are free at the time of posting, as well as some bargain e-books with reduced prices!

E-Reader Perks

Our goal is simple: to help people who love to read discover fabulous, new-to-them authors. If you are an author and your book is going to be temporarily free on the Amazon, Kobo, and/or Barnes and Noble websites, use our contact form to get in touch; we will help you spread the word!

Free Kindle Books & Tips

If you are an author and would like to have your book promoted (for free) on our site, please fill out the form below: your book must be free in the Amazon Kindle Store and must have an average user rating of at least 4 out of 5 stars for consideration. Please note each book submitted cannot be promoted due to space limitations on a particular day, but if your book is selected we will contact you at the email address you provide below.

GalleyCat Facebook Page

You can post your book in our New Books section, an easy way to share your book with our readers.

Goodkindles

We are a place where you post your own article about your title and can reach the readers. We do not review your book–we give you a platform to tell everyone what do you think is most interesting about your book and what you think will interest readers so much that they will go and buy your book.

Meet Our Authors Forum

A place on Amazon where writers can talk about their work.

Kindle Mojo

A full fledged social media site for Indie Authors and now — for their readers as well.

Flurries of Words

Reader's Site for Book Reviews, Flash Fiction, Interviews, Freebies, Free & Bargain e-books and Much More . . .

Books on the Knob

Book reviews and bargain reads, along with games, music, computers, and technology now and again.

Free-booksy

Have a permafree book or a KDP Select promotion coming up? The Free-booksy Feature gets your book in front of thousands of voracious readers, the surest way to boost downloads. Your book must be free in order to qualify for a Free-booksy Feature.

Online Book Club

Author Dashboard is the section of the website where you can manage your review requests, view the Author FAQ, upload review copies, and access our other cool services for authors.

The Book Marketing Network

For book authors, self-publishers, publishers, publicists, e-book authors, and others involved in writing, publishing, and marketing e-books.

http://ereadergirl.com/

Just what it sounds like — reviews from a gal.

Living Parables of Central Florida

Living Parables of Central Florida Living Parables of Central Florida, Inc., of which EABooks Publishing is a division, supports Christian charities providing for the needs of their communities. Ministries are encouraged to join hands and hearts with like-minded charities to better meet unmet needs in their communities. Annually the Board of Directors chooses the recipients of seed money to facilitate the beginning stages of these charitable activities.

Mission Statement

To empower start up, nonprofit organizations financially, spiritually, and with sound business knowledge to participate successfully as a responsible 501(c)3 organization that contributes to the Kingdom work of God.

Incubator Program

The goal of the Incubator Program: The Small Non-Profit Success Incubator Program, provides a solid foundation for running a successful non-profit through a year-long coaching process, eventually allowing these charities to successfully apply for grants and loans from others so they can further meet unmet needs in their communities.

Made in the USA
Columbia, SC
16 April 2022

59067903R00104